RIVER OF LIFE

by

JAMES S. STEWART

ABINGDON PRESS
Nashville and New York

RIVER OF LIFE

Copyright © 1972 by James S. Stewart

Library of Congress Cataloging in Publication Data

STEWART, JAMES STUART, 1896- . 1. Presbyterian Church—Sermons.

2. Sermons, English—Scotland. I. Title.

BX9178.S7917R58   252'.05'2   72-2031

ISBN 0-687-36480-9

MANUFACTURED BY THE PARTHENON PRESS AT
NASHVILLE, TENNESSEE, UNITED STATES OF AMERICA

To
Helen and Hilary
and John
with love

ACKNOWLEDGMENTS

A few of these studies have already appeared in print, and for permission to include them here I am grateful to the editors and publishers of *The Expository Times, Man's Dilemma and God's Answer* (S.C.M. Press) and *Best Sermons*, ed. Dr. Paul Butler (Van Nostrand).

CONTENTS

Who can faint while such a river
  Ever flows their thirst to assuage,
Grace which, like the Lord the Giver,
  Never fails from age to age?
JOHN NEWTON

There is a river, the streams whereof make
  glad the city of God.
THE PSALMIST

I

RIVER OF LIFE

'Every thing shall live whither the river cometh'—Ezekiel 47:9.

Here was Ezekiel in Babylon, dreaming of his fatherland across
the desert, his 'sweet and blessed country, the home of God's
elect'. Twenty-five long years he had lived in Babylon an exile,
but the flame of his passionate patriotism was burning still as
brightly as on that dreadful day of deportation when Nebuchadnezzar's soldiers had rounded up their batch of captives and
marched them out through the Jerusalem gates. How vividly he
remembered it—the stricken hour of parting, the last glimpse of
the City of God before the road had rounded the bend of the
hill and hid it from his eyes for ever! Twenty-five years before
—and here he was still dreaming of his homeland. Still all the
western windows of his being were flung wide open every day
towards Jerusalem:

> I vow to thee, my country—all earthly things above—
> Entire and whole and perfect, the service of my love.

Still the very dust of Zion to this man was dear: the very ruins
and rubble of the once magnificent temple where as a young
priest Ezekiel himself had ministered, loving every detail of the
temple worship, the very stones of the city's wrecked battlements
and burnt-out buildings and deserted streets, were a magnet to
draw his heart. He could have made his own the moving words
of the Hebrew poet of the captivity: 'By the rivers of Babylon,
there we sat down; yea, we wept when we remembered Zion ...
If I forget thee, O Jerusalem, let my right hand forget her cunning; ... if I prefer not Jerusalem above my chief joy.' Twenty-
five years of Babylon, and still—'Where your treasure is, there
will your heart be also.'

> Jerusalem, my happy home,
> Would God I were in thee!
> Would God my woes were at an end,
> Thy joys that I might see!

That is the background of this great sequence of visions at the close of Ezekiel's book. They came to him on the anniversary day of the destruction of Jerusalem by Nebuchadnezzar's armies. At the beginning of chapter 40, the prophet is careful to give the precise date of the final series of visions: it was on the anniversary of Judah's darkest hour. Those who have sorrow-laden commemorative days in their own year will understand his feelings then.

But watch what happened. Suddenly as in a dream he is caught up by the Spirit of the Lord. He feels himself transported beyond the western wilderness. He is back in his beloved Judah. He is standing again on the rugged rock of Zion. He sees the city spread out before him, no longer wretched and shattered and deserted, but splendid and stately and thronged with citizens. He sees the temple resurrected from its ruins, with a magnificence outvying the dreams of Solomon. He sees the glory of the Lord which had departed on the evil day coming back tenfold more glorious. And he sees the river.

This is the feature of his vision that draws our thoughts today: the river rising on the temple rock, beneath the very altar of God; descending to the plain and to the desert, deepening and expanding as it goes; bringing as it flows through that burning, blistered waste of wilderness eastward from Jerusalem, bringing everywhere healing and fertility and life; bursting at last a mighty rushing torrent into the Dead Sea, sweetening even those brackish waters of death. 'Everything shall live whither the river cometh.'

There are pedantic commentators who have tried to tell us that the whole picture is fantastic and geographically impossible. How could the river rise beneath the altar? How, in the absence of any tributaries, could it deepen so rapidly that within a mile and a half of its source it was quite unfordable—'waters to swim in'? How could it get past the steep limestone ridge that separates Jerusalem on the east from the Dead Sea, defying the physiographical contour of the land as though great mountain barriers did not exist? These questions, over which prosaic commentators shake their solemn heads, never troubled Ezekiel. The prophet has more urgent business on his mind and heart than details of geography. For this is the river of life, whose course is set by God alone. This is the great stream of supernatural grace to fertilise a thirsty, haggard world. This is the soul-refreshing experience, for lack of which multitudes today are going through life restless and frustrated and dissatisfied and thirsty for they know not what. This is the surge and power of the Spirit, pouring out across the barren scene of human misery, corruption, sin and death, to give healing, hope, renewal, life. And 'everything shall live whither the river cometh'.

You can see, then, that even if the Holy Spirit is not mentioned explicitly anywhere in this passage, He is none the less here in every word of it. And is there anything we need more—anything a wounded world needs more for the healing of its hurt, anything a languid Church needs more for the vitalising of its faith, anything our own dull, defeated lives, our conventionally religious lives, need more to make them alert, dynamic and victorious, than a new baptism in these waters of Ezekiel, a new submersion in the Spirit? 'There is a river, the streams whereof make glad the City of God', and reclaim the wilderness of the world. 'Everything shall live whither the river cometh.'

Now from the mass of symbolism in the prophet's vision let us single out just one or two salient points.

Notice, first, that *the river came down from the heights*. The stream which was to irrigate the plain and fertilise the desert had its source away up in the rugged hills of Zion.

Do you see what that is telling us, for our own situation today? It is surely telling us this—that God alone can give the power to make a better world. Down from the heights of the divine must come the inrush of creative energy—else all our plans are vain.

So much of our planning today is on the purely horizontal level. It is thinking in terms of a one-dimensional existence. It is still stubbornly believing, despite all the evidence to the contrary, that man is the master of his fate and the sole architect of his destiny: that human ideals—a little more goodwill, a little more knowledge, education, social science, conservation, group dynamics, decent housing, economic reorganisation—can by themselves transform the desert into a garden of the Lord.

Let us be fair to the vast amount of worthy and enriching planning going on today. We need it all. We need far more, not less, social involvement and concern. But let us not forget that river tumbling from the heights!

The people who are content to live in the realm of the natural and the human tend to think of life and history as a long, flat, level process. Here, in the middle, is the present moment; there on one side is the past; there on the other is the future, stretching far away, with the perfect world, the final Utopia, somewhere at the end. This is life in one dimension.

And that is what the Bible, on every page of it, challenges and denies. 'If you live like that,' says the Bible, 'you are blind! You are missing nine-tenths of the truth. For this present moment and all those fleeting moments, which you see only as infinitesimal links in the long chain binding the future to the past, are far more than that: they are the dwelling-place of God. And this natural, human, horizontal level on which our lives are lived is all the time being intersected and invaded by the unseen and eternal!'

That fact, for those who come awake to it, is surely the most revolutionary, explosive fact in all the world. It was the clear realisation of this stupendous fact—a fact which, as the event proved, had enough spiritual dynamite in it to turn the world upside down—which explains the irrepressible excitement of early Christianity. And not its excitement only, but also its strength, its effectiveness, its drive. They knew, those men, that God was in the field when He was most invisible. They stammer with excitement when they try to describe it. They are consumed with their eagerness to share it.

And the point is—it is still true. It is true for this broken and frustrated world. It is true for the Church, so often puzzled by its seeming lack of impact on society. It is true for the most despairing and defeated soul amongst us now. This is the wonderful news of Pentecost.

May we not trace the root of our disenchantment to this—

that we have been trying to live the Christian life without the necessary equipment: like a man trying to do a round-the-world voyage rowing? And of course it cannot be done. You cannot live Christ's kind of life in your own strength. You cannot do something which is essentially supernatural with purely natural resources. You can, if God adds on an extra capacity: like the man who circles the world flying. And the gospel says that the extra capacity, the supernatural, spiritual capacity, is really and truly available.

Let us get this clear by facing the alternatives. Here they are. Either the creative God can come right into our lives, or else He can't. Either the word 'spiritual' is the most terrific word in our vocabulary, and the thing it stands for the most dynamic reality in life, or else the whole make-up of religion is sophistry and sham. Either you and I can have the baptism of eternity, you and I with all our defeats and disappointments, often like the disciples toiling all night and taking nothing, can taste now the very life of God: or else Jesus spoke falsely. You will not say, will you, that Christ deceived you? Therefore fear not—only believe! The power is there, for you, for me, for all the world, the very power in which Jesus and the apostles lived: and there is only one requirement—that our hearts should be really set upon it, yearning for it enough to make a surrender of the will to Christ in decisive self-commitment. Of course we don't normally want it like that, do we? And yet, and yet—sometimes in our best moods we do. 'Lord, I believe: help Thou mine unbelief.' Lord, I repent: help Thou my impenitence. Lord, I commit myself to Thee: help Thou my shrinking from commitment.

This, for the Church and for all of us, is the crucial issue, and I wish I could have put it to you more clearly. But God's Spirit will tell you in your own hearts. Let us move on.

Ezekiel saw the river of life descending from the heights to the thirsty plain. The power must come from above. But he does not leave it at that. His vision was more precise. The river he saw *issued from the temple*. Its source was beneath the altar. It came out from the courts of the Lord's House.

Do you not feel the challenge of that symbolism? It means

that the Church, for all its faults, for all its glaring, disconcerting
faults, is still right on the line of the divine purpose for humanity.
It is still the point at which God, seeking to remake the world,
can most readily take hold by His Spirit. It is the instrument God
plans to use.

Can we think of that, and then look with equanimity at the
Church as it exists today? The river that is to heal the world,
said Ezekiel, comes out from the temple. Does it indeed?

In the apostolic age, yes, certainly. For then the whole Church
was throbbing with the urge and impetus of its glorious mission.
These men were facing the world with good news, not good
advice. They were not in those days blasé about their holy things.
They were not so busy with the techniques of service that they
had no time for worship, wonder, adoration. They were not a
dull debating-club, nor even a mildly benevolent human agency
with pious good intentions towards their fellow men. They were
a conquering divine society, with a startling and magnificent
vitality, exhilaratingly alive with the very life of the risen Jesus.
And that is why, literally, they rejuvenated a world grown old
and cold and weary. The river rose in the temple.

Does it still today? In the Church? The river for the healing
of the world? God wills that it should. And if the Church should
grow lethargic and Christendom complacent and composed; if
the sense of a terrible urgency dies out of the Church's message,
and men hear no longer the pleading and the passion of the
Christ; if our congregations are not providing the young men
and women needed to go into all the world and take the gospel
by word and action to every creature; if our Church members
are not realising that their Christian mandate is to be witnesses,
and that if they are not witnessing, their faith is stagnant and of
no avail; if the Church is content to go on purveying to the world
outside its doors only what that world can in any case get else-
where, and get far better; if the Christian fellowship is not
fulfilling its high calling to be a community of the resurrection,
the bearer of new life—it is a denial of Christ every whit as
blatant as Simon Peter's when he said 'I know not the Man':
and judgment must begin at the House of God. For God has
committed to His Church—that is, to you and me—the possession of the gospel, the glorious tidings which are the lost world's

only hope. Breathe on us, Breath of God! On us in the Church send resurrection: that the world may know that in Christ is life, and the life is the light of men!

Pass on to another salient feature of the vision. Did you notice *how Ezekiel's river deepened*—water to the ankles, to the knees, to the loins, waters at last to swim in? There is something wrong with our religious experience if it is not an ever-deepening tide. Within a mile and a half of its source, Ezekiel's river was too deep for any crossing. A mile and a half! Look back on your own earthly pilgrimage. Reckon up the mounting miles that have been traversed since consciously you committed your life to Christ and His discipleship. Has it been a deepening river? A growing knowledge of God? An always increasing surprise, a fresh unwearied wonder at the grace and power of Christ? Some of us with sorrow would have to confess that the stream which began, perhaps thirty or forty miles back, is but a meagre, scanty little rivulet still, and that never once in our religious lives have we known what it could mean—in Ezekiel's phrase—to have 'waters to swim in'. Perhaps some would even say—'The stream that sprang sparkling from beneath the altar of the temple of the Lord on the day of my first Communion is only a memory for me: it died out miles back yonder among the sands and rocks of life, and only the dry, empty channel is left to show where a river ought to have been.'

But it does not need to be like this. Ezekiel's vision is sent by God for you. 'Son of man,' said the angel to the prophet, as they stood together beside those rising waters, 'hast thou seen this?' Have you understood it? This is not a fictitious picture, a rhetorical irrelevance. It is the substantive truth of our holy religion: from strength to strength, from insight to insight, from glory to glory; from the love for Christ you have today to a still more burning passion of devotion tomorrow; from this year's certainty of God to next year's still more impregnable conviction—the river deepening with every mile! It is not pretence. It really happens.

And the secret? There is only one secret I know, and it is this. Keep in the fellowship of Jesus. Keep going back far oftener to the manger, the cross, the empty tomb. Stand with Peter on the shore listening to His voice. Kneel with Mary Magdalene at His feet. Climb the hill outside the city wall. Run with those two breathless disciples to the tomb on Easter morning. Keep looking on Him, orientating your life towards Him, identifying yourself with the will of God revealed in Him. His Spirit will do the rest. From the dried-up channels of the soul there will come again the sound of the deep waters and the rising tide.

It is a wonderful thing to know that even if you have been a Christian for forty, fifty years or more you can be making discoveries about Jesus Christ today that you never knew before.

> Who can faint while such a river
> Ever flows their thirst to assuage,
> Grace which, like the Lord the Giver,
> Never fails from age to age?

And so we finish where Ezekiel finished. *'Everything shall live whither the river cometh.'* He sees the Judean desert, burnt bare and haggard in the merciless heat, springing into life because the river of the Lord has crossed it. He sees even the Dead Sea itself, that sweltering rift in the earth, that 'bit of the infernal regions come up to the surface', as one traveller has described it, 'hell with the sun shining into it', he sees even that transfigured utterly; those deadly, brackish waters in which no life can exist so healed and sweetened that the fishermen can now ply their craft from one end of the Sea to the other.

In other words, he sees that so marvellous is the power of God's Spirit to heal and bless, that wherever that Spirit comes all things are possible. Everything lives—the devastation of the world, the society secularised into paganism, the minds corrupted with a false philosophy; everything lives—the Church half-suffocated sometimes with its own ecclesiasticisms, the souls gone stale and stagnant, the religion deadened and conventionalised into mere respectability; everything lives—our own so often frustrated and defeated lives, our youthful hopes and visions and ideals vanished in the ravages of time and the wreckage of the years, our own spiritual impotence and deadness of heart—everything lives where the river comes!

Is this possible? Or is it just a mocking dream? Is it like the dream of the medieval physicians and philosophers who spent their days trying to find the elixir of life, some draught of living water which would rejuvenate and recreate anyone growing old and weary and burdened with the years, and would guarantee eternal youth? Of course all their dreaming and research proved futile. They all grew old and died, and never found it.

But is there not a luminous word of Jesus declaring that, in the deepest sense of all, this elusive, miracle-working potion for which the philosophers of ancient time searched in vain is indeed no mocking dream? It does exist. 'In the great day of the feast, Jesus stood and cried, saying, If any man thirst, let him come unto Me, and drink.' It is thus that Ezekiel's vision is taken up into and crowned by the vision of the seer of the Book of Revelation: 'He shewed me a pure river of water of life, clear as crystal, proceeding out of the throne of God and of the Lamb.' It is no dream or fantasy. It is the most certainly available and verifiable of realities: Christ's great rejuvenating gift to every thirsty soul, the elixir of life eternal, here and hereafter.

Do you want it? Does the Church want it? The sometimes tired and jaded Church? Is the Church as we know it today crying out for the baptism of Christ's Spirit, as a land that is thirsty cries out for the great rain? Does it want this miracle, this exhilaration of vision and conviction and zeal perpetually renewed, this ringing shout athwart the long centuries of its missionary pilgrimage towards the ultimate consummation—'Arise, shine, for thy light is come, and the glory of the Lord is risen upon thee'? And do you and I want it? This vitality, this God-possession, this rejuvenating joy and power and poise and peace? Who could not want it? And you know the conditions: faith, prayer, meditation on the Word, fellowship with Christ in the Sacraments, commitment to His mission in the world. You know the conditions. And so do I. And the only question is—what are we going to do about it, now that we know?

For it is all true. It is true for you, this very moment. 'Whosoever will, let him take the water of life freely.'

II

THE CROSS AS POWER AND WISDOM

'The Jews require a sign, and the Greeks seek after wisdom: but we preach Christ crucified, unto the Jews a stumbling-block, and unto the Greeks foolishness; but unto them which are called, both Jews and Greeks, Christ the power of God, and the wisdom of God'— 1 Corinthians 1:22-24.

There are two demands we often make on God, in face of the tragic element of life and all the mystery of the world. The one is intervention, the other interpretation.

Intervention, action—this first. 'Let God do something! If He is really a God of righteousness, let Him prove it. If He is sovereign in His universe, let Him demonstrate His sovereignty. Why should a hurricane in the Caribbean, an earthquake in Japan, a famine in India, devastate ten thousand homes, and God give no sign? Why should man's inhumanity to man and the endemic injustice of the world sabotage the dream of progress? Why should nuclear devilry threaten the extinction of the world? Let God arise, and let His enemies be scattered!' Intervention—that is the first demand.

The second is interpretation, explanation. 'If only we could make sense out of life's jumbled pattern!' Some time ago I had a letter from a young doctor in America. She was working in a children's hospital where babies are sometimes brought in suffering from fatal disease. 'What am I to say to these parents?' she asked me. 'When they demand, "Where is the sense, the providence, the rationality of this?" what am I to answer?' We have all felt the cutting edge of that enigma. If only there were some clue to the riddle! If only providence would explain!

These are two great demands we are constantly making on God—intervention, interpretation.

Now here is an immensely significant fact: these were precisely the demands being made when the Christian faith first launched itself upon the world. 'The Jews require a sign, and the Greeks seek after wisdom.'

'The Jews require a sign'—that is, action, intervention, a visible demonstration of God's power. That is what the Jew wants, says Paul. That is characteristic of the Jewish attitude to life. 'Let God assert Himself visibly, dramatically. Let Him make bare His holy arm in the eyes of all the nations. Let Him deal with the dictators, and ruin the aggressors. Let Him in the twinkling of an eye eliminate incurable disease and heartbreak and all the sorrow and injustice of the world.' 'Awake,' cries Isaiah, 'put on strength, O arm of the Lord!' 'The Jews require a sign.'

'And the Greeks seek after wisdom'—that is, a rational interpretation and explanation of the divine purpose. That is what the Greek wants, says Paul. That is characteristic of the Greek attitude to life—always dissecting ultimate questions; always fashioning some new philosophy to rationalise the chaos and make this unintelligible life coherent; always searching for the solving word, the hidden pattern, the correct intellectual formula —and imagining sometimes it has found it in some early Greek version of logical positivism, linguistic analysis, depth psychology, or a clever blue-print of a new order. 'The Greeks seek after wisdom.'

So, you see, the situation Paul is addressing is not an old Bible story. It is our situation precisely. It is right in the centre of the contemporary map. That Jew demanding a sign, a divine intervention, is just ourselves. That Greek seeking after wisdom, interpretation, is just ourselves. We are all in this together.

Now watch what follows. Paul here asserts that God has faced exactly these two demands, and given His answer. And God's answer to both of them is the same. It is the answer of the cross. 'We preach Christ crucified.' 'There, Jew, is your "sign"—the divine dramatic deed you clamour for. And there, Greek, is your "wisdom"—the solving word for the whole baffling enigma.' All roads lead to Calvary at last.

But now the question is—what do you think of that for an answer? I have said that the Jew and the Greek are just ourselves. So we had better see what the Jew and the Greek thought of the answer.

The Jew certainly did not think much of it. Paul tells us that. 'We preach Christ crucified—unto the Jews a stumbling-block.' The word is *skandalon*, a scandal, an embarrassing, shocking offence.

Now of course Paul knew what he was talking about. For Paul was a Jew himself. He had felt just like that once upon a time when he contemplated the cross. The thing is a scandal! So Saul of Tarsus felt. For the Messiah of the Jews was to be a warrior-king. He was to ride through rivers of blood to the conquest of the world. Ride on, ride on in majesty! God save the King! O King, live for ever! But this Man upon a gallows —a scandal indeed! Did not the law of Moses say—'Cursed is everyone who hangs on a tree'? 'Take it away,' cried the Jew. 'I want a demonstration of power, and you give me this pathetic symbol of weakness and defeat, this broken, tortured, thorn-crowned victim, nailed hand and foot, helpless. Strange token of omnipotence this! God with His back to the wall! You have given me the exact opposite of my demand. I wanted power, inter-vention—you have given me impotence and discomfiture. A stumbling-block indeed! Take it away.'

And we are stumbled by it too—are we not?—we who clamour for our twentieth-century sign, who think that God—if there be a God—should force His will upon recalcitrant dictators and incurable disease and all the stubborn intractability of the world: 'Put on strength, O arm of the Lord!' And what we see instead is that gaunt tree on Golgotha, love crucified there, and crucified still in a thousand thousand innocent sufferers. 'Jesus,' said Pascal, 'will be in agony till the end of the world.' A stumbling-block indeed! 'Don't look at that picture, you fool,' cries one Dostoievsky character to another who is gazing at a picture of the crucifixion. 'Don't you know a man can lose his faith by look-ing at that picture?' 'Yes,' comes the answer, 'that is just what is happening to me.' Christ crucified—a stumbling-block, a scandal. That is the Jew.

What of the Greek? What did he think of God's answer?

The Greek did not think much of it. Paul tells us that also. 'We preach Christ crucified—unto the Greeks foolishness.' The word is *moria*, sheer absurdity.

Again Paul knew what he was talking about. For Paul had in him a considerable element of the Greek, the cosmopolitan. He had felt just like that in the old days, contemplating the cross. Folly! So Saul of Tarsus had reacted. For the Saviour the Greeks looked for was to be the apotheosis of all the culture and philosophy of the world. He was to be a super-Aristotle, a demigod for wisdom, the head of a new intellectual aristocracy. But this crucified Man, this

> Sacred Head, sore wounded,
> With grief and shame bowed down—

'Take it away!' cried the Greek. 'I want a rational explanation, and in the name of all that is irrational you offer me this! It offends my aesthetic temperament. It insults my cultured intelligence. A gallows—it is so undignified. You have given me the exact opposite of my demand. I wanted interpretation, explanation—you have given me only deeper discord and anomaly, confusion worse confounded. It is sheer absurdity! Take it away.'

And we are there too, are we not, with our perpetual 'Why?' Why is life so unjust? Why is suffering so indiscriminate? Every minister in his pastoral counselling knows these questions which, however often he tries to answer them, drain the virtue out of him. Why did my beloved die? Why could I never realise my heart's desire? Why is it so difficult to believe in God? Why is the pathway to maturity so slow and painful and humbling and bewildering? Why are there so many complications along the road?

And instead of light, it looks—this cross of Calvary—like deeper darkness: instead of the dawn of the kingdom of heaven, Christ descending into hell. Is it not mad to offer this as the clue to the mystery of life and the riddle of the world? We preach Christ crucified—to the Greeks sheer folly.

But wait! This is where the sudden exciting hopefulness of the gospel appears. Those immediate, instinctive reactions of

Jew and Greek to the cross were not the last word then—nor are they the last word now.

For that Jew requiring a sign, a demonstration of power, and finding only a stumbling-block, has a second look at the cross, then a third, then a fourth, perhaps a hundredth. He is going deeper. He is changing his verdict. And suddenly, 'I see it!' he cries, 'it was true after all! I wanted God to act, and—how blind I was!—this cross which I called a stumbling-block, a scandal, of all God's mighty acts this is the mightiest! Here is the victory that conquers the world. Here is the devil's strategy defeated!'

This is the great discovery. Do let us try to get it clear today. I would put it to you like this.

The really damnable thing about evil is its self-propagating power. Injury produces resentment, resentment produces retaliation, this produces further injury, that produces further pain and evil: and so the whole miserable story drags on hopelessly for ever. This is the devil's standard strategy, individually and collectively—and it is frightfully successful: it is the vicious circle that could easily have spelt the ruin of the world.

But now look! When Christ died on the cross, forgiving, He broke right into that process. He met this whole tyranny of evil, and outmanoeuvred it. For here at last was One who refused to allow injury and pain to produce resentment. Instead, He took all the pain and injury into His own body and soul. Thus in His broken body and soul He absorbed it, neutralised it, cut short its power. This is the frustration of the devil. This is the atonement of the world.

I put it to you: there is not one of us today who believes that in the presence of the cross of Christ we are in the presence of defeat. We know we are in the presence of victory. Here is the cross, history's blackest crime—and history's brightest hope. Here is the most atrocious tragedy ever enacted—and it is precisely this which has become the supreme assurance of the sovereignty of God. They gave Him a cross, and He made it a throne. They slammed every door against Him, and flung Him outside the city gates to die; and that very act has lifted up the gates of the universe to let the King come in. They thought they had hunted God to His doom, not knowing that it was God who was tracking them down. He reigns from the tree. 'We preach Christ crucified, the power of God'—the one power big enough to take a grip of the world's desperate situation, and defy the gates of hell, and give a fresh start to humanity. If only the world today would align itself with Jesus in His victory, we should see the powers of darkness discomfited again.

Do you see where this touches your life and mine? I am not suggesting, mark you, that God wants us quietly to acquiesce in evils and scourges that can and should be removed. No, surely God wants His human race to be rebels and fighters against needless suffering and incurable disease, to fight these things with all the resources of knowledge and science and dedicated life until they are swept for ever from the earth. That is different. But suppose there is some trouble in your life that cannot be removed. Suppose there is some overwhelming enigma of desolating sorrow—as with those parents in the children's hospital about whom my friend wrote to me. Suppose there is some heavy trial you are bearing now. Suppose there is the sting of sin to make you miserable and ashamed: 'O wretched man that I am! Who shall deliver me?' And suppose you were to get your life into the way of that power of the cross, that alchemy that can turn the iron of bitterness into the gold of blessing. If it is going to heal mankind at last, and bring the harvest of the divine purpose out of the wreck and ruin of the world, do you not think it could perhaps help to heal you here and now? Even with all the monotony of defeat, the accusing voices, the bungling and the disappointment, do you not think that union with this Christ could do the miracle for us now? It is worth believing. I do not know how to fathom by any theory of atonement what it was that happened at Calvary. I do not know how deep were the waters crossed, nor how dark the night the Lord passed through. I only know that through those deep waters and that dark night the Shepherd found His sheep. I only know that John Bunyan was speaking for ten thousand times ten thousand when he said that at the sight of the cross the burden fell off Christian's back and was never seen again. I only know that when they thrust Jesus outside their city gates to die they were putting the keys of the whole world into His pierced hands for ever. 'We preach Christ crucified, the power of God.'

Finally, what of the Greek? The Greek, searching after wisdom and interpretation and explanation, and finding only foolishness —he too has a second look at the cross, then a third, then a fourth, perhaps a hundredth. He is going deeper. He is going deeper into the heart of things than his own Plato and Aristotle ever went. He is seeing right across the frontier into another world. And suddenly, 'I see it!' he cries, 'it was true after all! I wanted God to explain, to interpret, and—how blind I was!— this cross that I called rank folly and absurdity, it is the word from heaven!'

For this is the ground-plan of the universe. This is the great Architect's design for building His new creation. This is the wisdom which created man at the first, and now at the cross it is creating the new humanity.

Are there not traces of this sometimes to be found even on the human level? A servant of Christ, working in a dreadful slum, takes in to share his humble abode a man who has been in trouble with the police for a stabbing affray. Folly? By any secular standard, rank folly. But what if it is the wisdom of God by which that broken life is to be remade? There was the head-master of a London school who, during an air attack, shepherded all the children into the safety of the shelters; and then, going back again to make doubly certain that no one had been left behind, was himself caught by a bomb and killed instantly. Was that sacrifice needless folly? Or was it perhaps the wisdom of God by which honour comes into its heritage?

These are only dim analogies, distant and remote. Here stands the cross of Jesus. Here is the sign that gives the lie to the plausible wisdom of material security. We are being told today that scientific humanism holds the key to security. We are being told that words like faith and providence are now unintelligent sentimentalities which we must leave out of the reckoning. We are even told that as long as we can build bigger and better ballistic missiles than other nations nothing else matters: this is our best security. What a hope! Men today are beginning to see through that decrepit philosophy. For in fact it is the bankrupt logic of fatalism and despair: 'mind at the end of its tether', to use H. G. Wells' phrase. Here stands the cross of Jesus—this essential insecurity, this foolishness of faith, this hope strained to the breaking-point, this love despised and rejected. This is the wisdom of God. And it is quite certain that life will work no other way.

Let me make this quite personal. Someone may say, 'Sacrifice? I don't want sacrifice. I am sick of the sound of the word. I am bored with Christianity's reiteration about taking up a cross. It is such a dismal dirge, such an outmoded ethic. Self-realisation —that is my goal: to be the arbiter of my own destiny, going ahead and fulfilling even what Christianity would tell me was an unfulfilable desire.'

But I am only asking you to look into your heart and look up at the cross. Does not your own heart tell you that the wisdom of God is there, and that life will work no other way? Canon Streeter once put it memorably: 'The primrose path of dalliance is early overrun with briars; and if we must be pierced with thorns, it is more kingly to wear them as a crown.' More kingly, yes, and infinitely more satisfying too. For Christ will be there to help and strengthen you; and, as Principal David Cairns used to say, 'What God did with the cross of His first-born Child Jesus, He can do with all the crosses of all His other children.' He can make them shine with glory.

When you reach that point in your thinking—'Christ crucified the wisdom of God'—suddenly it flashes upon you, 'I must be in this with Jesus. I must be identified and united with Him in His sacrifice and passion—in that self-offering of which the dear Lord said, "To this end was I born, and for this cause came I into the world."' He is bearing now, this very hour, the shame and suffering of all the earth. And I know He is looking round on me and saying, 'Will you stand in and share with Me in this, or is it nothing to you?' For today Christ, the Power and the Wisdom of God, stands at the door and knocks. While the sands of time are running out, and the hurrying hours mould our destiny, He stands at the door and knocks. It is so urgent that we should make our dedication real.

> Passionately fierce the voice of God is pleading,
>   Pleading with men to arm them for the fight;
> See how those hands, majestically bleeding,
>   Call us to rout the armies of the night.

Bread of Thy Body give me for my fighting,
Give me to drink Thy Sacred Blood for wine,
While there are wrongs that need me for the righting,
While there is warfare splendid and divine.

This is your calling. This is your vocation. To this end were you born, and for this cause you came into the world.

III

LORD OF THE HARVEST

'A sower went out to sow his seed ...
The seed is the word of God ...
The seed in good soil represents those who bring a good and honest heart to the hearing of the word, hold it fast, and by their perseverance yield a harvest'—Luke 8: 5-15 (N.E.B.).

It is clear that the incomparable words of this parable are a transcript of Christ's own experience. This was Jesus thinking aloud about His own success and failure with the souls of men. Might not God's harvest have been richer? Could not the yield have been greater? Why should human torpor, stolidity and unresponsiveness baffle the love of heaven?

If that was Christ's question then, it is our question still. 'Look at the world,' we say. 'Is this the harvest Christ hoped to see after the passion of two thousand years?' And we might add, if we are honest with ourselves, 'Look at our own hearts—why is God's harvest not ten times richer there?'

To bring this to a point: Who is to blame? Whose is the fault?

Observe that in the story Jesus told three factors were present: the Sower, the Seed, the Soil. Can we trace the fault to one of these?

The Sower. That is Jesus Himself: the Master evangelising Galilee.

We know what happened then. At first the thronging crowds, the tumultuous excitement, the heather on fire throughout the length and breadth of the land, the delirious enthusiasm, the cry 'What manner of man is this? We will take Him and make Him a King!' All that for a time: then—the waning popularity, the dwindling crowd, the hardening criticism, the boredom and indifference and unconcealed contempt. 'He will never make a new world for us—this unpractical idealist. Away with the false Messiah! He will see no harvest of His hopes.'

And so it was not only in His own lifetime. History has seen it repeated—the Church experiencing a flood-tide of revival that carried everything before it, so that Christians could feel it bliss in such a dawn to be alive: and then, the sudden ebb, the old formality and coldness and suffocating unheroic spiritual commonplaceness creeping back again.

Has the Sower failed? Has Christ miscalculated? Is this a possibility we have to reckon with?

Certainly we have to reckon with it when you reflect that all of us Christians are now meant—under Christ—to be sowers of the seed. Are we perhaps the reason why God's harvest in the secular world is not greater? If I as a minister of the gospel become defeatist, sowing doubts in people's minds instead of faith; if you, Christ's representatives in business and home, family circle and social set, are not eager and alert in Christian witness—it may well be the harvest will be a poor one. That is understandable. The sower has been found wanting.

But the difficulty is that here in the story the Sower is Christ Himself. Has He, then, failed?

You have only to mention that possibility to rule it out for ever. Christendom may have misrepresented Christ, we who are His Church may have falsified His image. But through all our pathetic bungling and blundering, that one Face still shines, the light and life of men. 'I find no fault in Him,' cried Pontius Pilate; and the whole world homologates that verdict still.

Once at a meeting in Hyde Park, London, an atheist lecturer ventured to attack the Founder of Christianity. He held up the central Figure of the Gospels to ridicule and what he thought was devastatingly clever caricature. But his audience, secular and unbelieving as many of them were, would not have it. Out from the crowd stepped a working man, strode up to the speaker and dared him to go on, and then turning to the crowd exclaimed —'Men, let's give three cheers for Jesus Christ!' And they gave them with a will. Crude? Yes, no doubt—yet magnificently right! For that gesture meant, You can vilify Christendom if you like, tear the Church to tatters, but—not a word against Christ! We find no fault in Him.

There, then, is the first part of our answer. If the harvest fails, it is not the fault of the Sower.

What of the second factor? Are we to trace the defect to the seed?

'The seed,' said Jesus, 'is the word of God.' That is to say, it is the message, the content of the gospel, the Fatherhood of God with the cross at the heart of it.

Is this conceivably the weakness? If the harvest is not richer, shall we blame it on the seed? Is this a possibility to be reckoned with?

Certainly it has to be reckoned with when we think that today the seed is what our Christian folk and Christian institutions are offering the world around our doors, the Church's interpretation or misinterpretation of the message. Is our version of the gospel perhaps the reason why God's harvest in the secular world is not greater? Yes, indeed, if we to whom the message has been committed have been in a hurry to adapt it to the temper of the times, capitulating to the spirit of the age to the extent of offering a God who is no longer transcendent Creator and personal Father but some abstract ground of being; a Saviour who is no more than humanity at its highest; a Holy Spirit so vague and metaphysical that no miracles are to be looked for any longer. How can we hope for a harvest then? That is understandable. The seed has been found wanting.

But again the difficulty is that here in the parable the seed is the gospel as Jesus Himself taught it, good news of God taking action in history to redeem His creation.

And the question is—if the harvest fails, shall we blame it on the seed?

Some indeed would say—'Yes, now you are getting near the truth. For this message of a cross on a Judean hill two thousand years ago and an empty tomb in a Jerusalem garden, a Father who knows every child and a home where we shall all meet at last —how in the wide world is that to meet the modern predicament or measure up to the sophisticated culture of western civilisation? In this space age, the thing is ludicrous and absurd. It just does not make sense.' 'Unto the Jews a stumbling-block, and unto the Greeks foolishness'—and to modern man come of age just meaningless.

Is that criticism sound? Has the seed failed? Was Jesus mistaken in His gospel? Again I submit that merely to ask that question is to answer it. For all down the centuries it is precisely this seed that in countless lives has sprung up to life eternal. I doubt not there are men in this church at this moment conquering the devil and learning to live nobly because God has met them at the cross. The message has been literally the greatest regenerative and transforming force in all the ages and in all the world.

Carlyle once walked with Emerson on a Scottish moor: and suddenly he stopped and gripped his companion's arm. 'Christ died on the tree,' he exclaimed, 'that built Dunscore kirk yonder —that brought you and me together.' Yes, and if anything is to bring men and nations together still, and storm and scatter the darkness of the world, it is that same luminous message that will do it: 'the power of God unto salvation'.

We now have the second part of our answer. When the yield at harvest disappoints, it is not the fault of the Sower, nor is it the fault of the seed.

What, then, of the third factor? What of the soil? Is the reason of the failure here?

Observe carefully how Jesus discriminates at this point. He differentiates certain kinds of soil.

There is a soil that is too hard. 'Some fell by the wayside.' It fell upon the beaten track, the path that ran around or across the field. That seed could not get in: it found no lodgment. The ground there was impervious.

'The beaten track'—do we not know that type of mind? The man who is set in his own opinions, who knows all the answers. The secular culture that is so enslaved by the slogans of the hour that the spiritual world cannot get at it. A whole generation who have heard so long about religion that they are quite impervious to it now. It simply does not penetrate. God may speak the word of eternal life, and it makes no impression. The seed falls on the beaten track, and the birds of the air carry it away.

Is there any help for that condition? Perhaps one day conceivably God may shatter that hardness with some sudden explosive dynamite of the Spirit. Otherwise the soil remains barren and unfruitful.

But if there is a soil that is too hard there is also, said Jesus, a soil that is too shallow. 'Some fell on stony ground' (this is Mark's version) 'where it had not much earth.' This soil looks promising; but beneath the narrow layer of earth, there is a hidden ridge of rock. Here the seed gets in and takes a grip, shooting up rapidly and making quite a show. But the layer of earth is too thin, the underlying rock too near the surface. There is no depth, no moisture. The swiftly accelerated growth is premature. The grain withers away.

'No depth of earth'—do you know that type of mind? It is here in the Gospels. It is the rich young ruler running to Christ, crying 'What must I do for eternal life?'—and then, when he was told what to do, turning round and going away sorrowful. It is that other demonstrative would-be disciple who accosted Jesus with effervescent enthusiasm: 'Lord, I will follow You wherever You go. I will go anywhere with You!' Then, when Jesus quietly answered, 'Foxes have holes, birds of the air have nests, but the Son of Man has nowhere to lay His head—will you follow Me now?'—the man, with his voluble rhetoric all punctured, turned and crept away. It is Bunyan's Mr. Pliable, brimming over with impassioned eagerness for the pilgrimage, pulling Christian by the sleeve: 'Come on, man, don't dawdle, let's mend our pace!'—but finding, at the first taste of difficulty, his bubbling eagerness suddenly evaporating: 'I've had enough. You can keep your Celestial City. I'm going home!'

'No depth of earth': it is the folk who respond to the contagion of a crowd and the emotion of a touching hymn and the glamour of a religious revival, but who lack the tenacity to stand fast in the faith when Christianity costs and the way of discipleship is hard.

'No depth of earth.' Perhaps this is the trouble with some of us today. Perhaps, when all is said and done, our religion is mostly on the surface still. Perhaps there is nothing we are needing so much as deepness of earth in our spiritual life.

Well, God has His own ways of deepening the shallow soil. Sometimes He drives a ploughshare of grief right through it. Sometimes He digs and delves with the instruments of discipline and affliction. The shallow soil, said Jesus, 'lacked moisture': sometimes the moisture God supplies is moisture of bitter tears. Yet, even so, must we not pray, like Masefield's Saul Kane watching the ploughman in the field in the grey light of morning— 'O God, do that for me! Whatever the cost, deepen Thou my spiritual life'?

> O wet red swathe of earth laid bare,
> O truth, O strength, O gleaming share,
> O patient eyes that watch the goal,
> O ploughman of the sinner's soul,
> O Jesus, drive the coulter deep
> To plough my living man from sleep.

The first soil was too hard, the second too shallow. But there is one other cause of spiritual failure noted in the parable. There is a soil that is too thorny. 'Some fell among thorns: and they choked it.' The seed sinks in, germinating and growing up to the harvest; but there are weeds and thistles keeping pace with it, threatening at last to stifle it and suffocate its life before the day of harvest home.

This indeed we know and understand. For the thorns, said Jesus, 'are the cares of this life', the worries and anxieties, the bewildering complexity of things, the daily distractions that keep clamouring at us and deafening us with their hectoring voice, the things seen and temporal that claim priority from our attention and rivet themselves upon our souls, yes, even the trivialities and inanities that go on bombarding our notice in advertising campaigns and on television screens—until our spiritual faculty, the thing within us that is made for God and is restless till it rests in Him, is well-nigh crushed and atrophied, and the eternal issues are crowded out. 'The thorns,' said Jesus, 'choke the word.'

Is that the trouble? Never forget, says Jesus here, that your spiritual life needs space and room to grow. It needs to be weeded out. It needs the light and air of heaven. It needs worship. It needs the bracing breath of the eternal. It is all wrong to make worship a matter of mood and chance and inclination, and church a place to go when there is nothing else to do. Worship is not that. It is a basic necessity of life, just like sunshine and fresh air and vitamins. And the reason why we get flurried and strained and hectic and neurotic, lacking in equilibrium and effectiveness and inner poise, is that we have been neglecting the basic need. We know in our hearts that this is true. We have been trying to live without our oxygen. And it is hopeless. It is absolutely impossible. Men and women, says Jesus here, make room in your daily life for God; weed out the things suffocating your higher existence: lest the thorny cares choke the word, and there be no harvest at the last.

Let me say finally this. Do not imagine that the total impression of this parable is sad and pessimistic, as though all the soil were bad. On the contrary, it is a piece of splendid optimism. The failures indeed are there, all over the field of human history— all the disappointments Jesus meets as He sows the seed in the soil of human hearts. But the failures are incidental to the ultimate success. The stress of the parable is not on the failures: it is on the abundant crop—'bearing fruit a hundredfold'. And the stress of the parable is on that, because the stress of the whole gospel is there.

We Christians are apt to take a terribly defeatist view of the situation sometimes. Perhaps it is understandable. But it is wrong. It is quite alien to the mind of Christ. Do not let us listen to the ecclesiastical pessimists who shake their solemn heads as though the Christian cause were losing out in the twentieth century. Not a shred of evidence for that: indeed, as Bishop Stephen Neill has been reminding us, all the world statistics show that the Christian mission has quadrupled itself since the century began. And do not let us think that the violence and cupidity and pornography and tension and revolt that fill the headlines today are the whole truth of the matter. Emphatically not! The whole point of Jesus' story is the good earth that did so splendidly.

No one ever looked out on this world so hopefully as Jesus Christ. Never for a moment—not even when they despised and rejected and finally killed Him—did He doubt that God's harvest was sure. 'If I be lifted up from the earth, I will draw all men unto Me.' Always that ringing confidence and audacious faith, always that shining certainty that God's sovereignty was no empty dream but a magnificent and triumphant reality!

And He had His evidence there before Him in Galilee—great multitudes of burdened folk for whom His coming meant the world made new; men and women who, once ashamed and defeated and spiritually dead, suddenly stood up and lived, because they had seen the Lord.

Sometimes the yield was literally 'thirtyfold, sixtyfold, a hundredfold'—and even incalculably more. What of that day when the risen Christ converted Saul of Tarsus? How many did Saul, Paul the apostle as he then became, win for the kingdom? The harvest of that one life was—not a hundredfold, more like ten thousandfold—or rather, because it is still going on, a thousand thousandfold, quite incalculable and immeasurable. This is the optimism of Christ.

And now today He looks at you and me. 'These are they', He says at the parable's end—and I wonder, are we included here?—'these are they who in an honest and good heart'—that means sincerity: Christ does not ask for faultless saints, He does ask that we should be sincere—'having heard the word, keep it'—that is personal appropriation, taking the word home to your heart, letting the seed get in—'and bring forth fruit with patience'—that is tenacity, for to grow a Christlike character is a progress as long as life itself, and never till we stand in the sunburst of eternal glory will the work be done.

Will God, then, win His harvest in you and me, and through us in the world? In our own strength, we can do nothing. We are feeble, helpless creatures. But Christ's power in us—breaking up the hard soil, deepening the shallow soil, cleansing the thorny soil—this can work the miracle, and make even God's dreams come true.

IV

THE FAITH THAT DEFIES DEFEAT

'Shadrach, Meshach, and Abednego answered and said to the king,
O Nebuchadnezzar, we are not careful to answer thee in this matter.
If it be so, our God whom we serve is able to deliver us from the
burning fiery furnace, and He will deliver us out of thine hand, O
king. But if not, be it known unto thee, O king, that we will not
serve thy gods, nor worship the golden image which thou hast set up'
—Daniel 3 : 16-18.

In days like the present, there are two attitudes of mind, two
opposite attitudes, against which every true Christian will be on
guard. One is complacency, the other is despair.

Complacency works in various directions.

There is the man who is complacent about the world. Talk to
him about the world's precarious plight, and he is not impressed,
or even is frankly impatient. 'Oh, do stop harping on about that,'
he retorts. 'Look on the bright side, believe in progress, and
remember the devil was dethroned long ago.'

Again, there is the Christian who is complacent about the
Church. No need, in his eyes, for the Church to repent in dust
and ashes: no need for Christendom to be called to contrition
and renewal. The Church is holding its own all right—let us con-
gratulate ourselves on that! Let us be at ease in Zion.

Once again, there is the Christian who is complacent about
himself, whose unspoken attitude is: 'I don't claim to be a
saint, but at least I am making a reasonably satisfactory show. I
reckon I am adequate to most of the demands life can make upon
me!'

This, in three dimensions, is the complacent Christian. And
he does not see that the world today is threatened by the most
deadly menace since the days of Nero; he does not see that the
Church needs desperately a baptism of fire and of the Holy

Spirit; he does not see that his own soul has scarcely begun its journey towards 'the measure of the stature of the fullness of Christ'.

But there is another equally dangerous attitude, the opposite attitude—despair. This also works in various directions.

There is the man who despairs about the world. 'How can I help it,' he asks, 'when this very generation has witnessed half the world engulfed by tyranny, liberty and democracy driven underground, perhaps smothered for ever?'

There is the Christian who despairs of the Church, who tells you frankly he does not see how anything as disunited as the Church, as inhibited by a gigantic credibility gap between practice and profession, as painfully and pathetically contaminated by the preposterous intrusiveness of the human element, can ever be the arm of Christ's strength or the tongue of Christ's Spirit. 'Son of man, can these bones live?'

And there is the Christian who despairs about himself. 'All very well,' he thinks, 'for Paul and John to talk about overcoming the world and being more than conquerors; but I am not like that. I am finished with these heroics. The game is not worth the candle. I need not try!'

It is against this twofold background—complacency on the one side, despair on the other—that this story in Daniel leaps to sudden life. I want you to feel the astonishing modernity of this story—which was born in the age of Antiochus and the Maccabees, Antiochus the foreign oppressor, and the Maccabees, the Jewish resistance movement. It is immensely relevant today.

There are just three factors in the story—Nebuchadnezzar, the image, and the furnace: and they are all contemporary facts. Nebuchadnezzar—we do not need to search far for him today: the spirit of a militant materialistic secularism, spectacularly rampant in its success, striding over half the earth. The image to be worshipped—we have this also: the subtle way in which secularism can disguise itself as a religion, the new twentieth-century Messiah, offering the most alluring, incredible gifts, something to fill the spiritual vacuum and elicit an almost mystical fervour and devotion. The burning fiery furnace—we have that too: the ultimate threat to all who refuse to conform to the spirit of the age. Collaborate, or go under! Conform, or be destroyed! This is the modernity of the book of Daniel.

And this is where we now look for our instruction at those three friends of Daniel, Shadrach, Meshach and Abednego, caught in that situation, standing in the context of Nebuchadnezzar, the image and the furnace. I ask you to notice two things about them.

First, this: whatever else they were, they were certainly not complacent. They had no illusions about the world, or the Church, or themselves.

They had no illusions about the world—the world that was focused in the person of Nebuchadnezzar. They knew there was something demonic here. Of course, they recognised his prowess. They admitted his constructive genius. They acknowledged the dynamism of his deification of the secular. But the price—and this these three men came to see with piercing clearness—was the enslaving of conscience: freedom of thought, speech, action, all gone. Here was a man wanting to be a god, and in the attempt he had become demonic. They had no illusions about Nebuchadnezzar, or about the world he represented.

Nor had they any illusions about the Church, the Church in this case being the people of Israel. Israel was in captivity precisely because of her sins. How fierce and colossal the might of Babylon, how puny the people of God!

Nor had they any illusions about themselves. That this crucial issue should have been focused in their persons was dreadful. Shadrach, Meshach, Abednego—

> The hopes and fears of all the years
> Are met in you tonight.

And, they wondered, who are we to be matched with God's great hour? 'Frail children of dust, and feeble as frail.' What if we break at the crucial hour? What if our nerve collapses?

No, they certainly were not complacent. And the first challenge of this story is that we should cast off complacency too.

It is time, for one thing, that we stopped having illusions about the world and the powers of darkness. 'We wrestle not against flesh and blood,' Paul told the Ephesians, 'we wrestle against far subtler unseen foes.' And Paul, if he were to come back today, and look out on this demon-possessed world, would surely say it more emphatically than ever. Of course, a secularist society can deny God and still do mighty works on earth. A materialist philosophy can achieve marvels on the technological level: it can even evince a certain pseudo-idealism, and speak to the aspirations of multitudes. But what are we to say when the God-denying, ultimately nihilistic way of life stands out in its true colours, with the threat to freedom, justice and humanity unmasked? We had better stop having illusions then.

Again, we had better have no illusions about Christendom and the Church. For can we be sure that our present troubles are not, in some sense, God's judgment on Christendom and the Church, for all the things they have left undone?

And finally, we had better have no illusions about ourselves. Who am I to bear the Christian name before the world? Who am I to be an advertisement of what the power of God can do? How dreadfully disappointed Christ must be!

So Shadrach, Meshach, Abednego were not complacent. That is the one thing. But—and this is the other—even less were they despairing.

They might have said, caught there between Nebuchadnezzar, the image and the furnace, 'This is the end, the bitter, unjust, hopeless end.' They might have said—

> The time is out of joint; O cursed spite
> That ever we were born to set it right.

But instead, sweeping the despair from their souls, they defied Nebuchadnezzar to his face. 'O king, we are not careful to answer thee in this matter—we need not waste one word in argument. Our God whom we serve is able to deliver us from the burning fiery furnace, and He will deliver us out of thy hand, O king!' And then, as if that were not fortitude and gallantry enough, comes this amazing thing: 'Our God can and will deliver us, *but if not*'—three words, the hammer that breaks the rocks in pieces and shatters the might of Babylon—'but if not, if we are not to be delivered, be it known to thee, O king, we will not serve thy gods or worship the golden image.'

Is it not magnificent? They did not say, with Jacob at Bethel and with so many of us at our prayers, 'If the Lord will look after me, then the Lord will be my God'—making a bargain with the Almighty. No. They said, with Habakkuk, 'Even if nothing should be left on earth, no fruit on the vine, no flocks in the field, nevertheless I will rejoice in God!' They did not say, 'I will trust Him to keep me safe from suffering.' They said, like Job, 'Though He slay me, yet will I trust in Him.' Not—'God is bound to avert the day of chaos'; but 'Even though chaos comes, God reigns!' Our God can deliver us; but if not—there are still absolute standards for which it is worth while to die. He can deliver us; but if not—there are still faith and loyalty and obedience to the will unseen. He can deliver us; but if not—we are still

> Safe though all safety's lost; safe where men fall;
> And if these poor limbs die, safest of all.

What a prophecy of Christ this story is! It points right across the centuries to the coming of the Son of Man. From the beginning of the ministry of Jesus to its end, was not this its setting—Nebuchadnezzar, the image, and the furnace? Right at the beginning, 'the devil took Him to an exceedingly high mountain, and showed Him all the kingdoms of the world and their glory. "All this will I give You, if You will fall down and worship me."' The kingship of the world—Yours for the taking, if You will collaborate with the world's ways and forget God's high demand. In a flash Jesus saw behind that shining promise the veiled threat if He should refuse—the seven-times-heated furnace of the cross. 'Get behind Me, Satan! God can deliver Me, God will deliver Me; but if not, I will not bow down to thee!' That stands right at the beginning of the story. And when you near the end, why was He so silent before His judges, Herod and Annas and Caiaphas and the rest? It is as though He were saying —'I am not careful to answer you, Herod, Annas, Caiaphas, in this matter. My Father can deliver Me. Has He not legions of angels at His beck and call? He can deliver Me. But if not, if this cup may not pass from Me, if the fiery furnace of Golgotha awaits, I will not compromise the truth and lose My soul!'

Still across the centuries that gallant 'But if not' of Shadrach, Meshach and Abednego, that divine 'But if not' of Christ, ring out like a thousand trumpets their brave defiance of despair. Can we make it ours? Yes, indeed, if we share the secret of their victory.

This is the crucial thing. What was their secret? What was it that enabled Daniel's companions to rise to that magnificent 'But if not' of faith?

Three things. Three words. Providence, Prayer, the Presence. Despair of the world? How could they, with their doctrine of providence? Despair of the Church? How could they, with their practice of prayer? Despair of themselves? How could they, with their experience of the unseen presence? And this is where the old story comes straight out of the page at you and me.

First, Providence. These three men had a profound insight into history, a deep reading of God's providential government of His universe. They saw that, if the powers of darkness had a lot of rope, still the end of the rope was in the hand of God. They saw that God in His sovereignty could use even what was pagan and demonic as the agent of His judgment and of His purifying of His people. They saw that even the empire of Nebuchadnezzar, the scourge of Israel, was, unknown to itself, an instrument in the hand of God, as Egypt had been before and Rome would be later. They saw that in the end God's great hour would strike and the demonism of Nebuchadnezzar be shattered, as Pharaoh had been shattered long before, and as Caesar would be in days to come. Even when the mailed fist of Babylon held Israel in a remorseless grip, they knew there was another Hand controlling and another Will. Therefore—'He can and will deliver us; but if not, if we have to perish ere deliverance comes, nevertheless, Nebuchadnezzar, we defy you, and glory to God in the highest!'

There stands the first secret of a conquering faith—Providence: this deep biblical insight into history, this prophetic reading of God's government of His universe. The earth is the Lord's and the fullness thereof; and even if the world sometimes seems careering to the devil, God still holds the reins. If evil

things lash Christendom and threaten ruin, it may indeed be a
judgment for what Christendom has left undone—the word
'crisis' means judgment—but it is a judgment of God, and the
day comes when God shatters the instrument of His judgment
and casts it away. Therefore, He can and will deliver us; but if
not, even if the worst should befall, even if Christendom as
we know it should be driven underground or blotted out, that
would not be the defeat of God: through that thick darkness
Christ would still be coming into His own; and blessed is He
who cometh in the name of the Lord—hosanna in the highest!

Providence—that was one secret of their victory. The second
was Prayer. They were men of prayer. The whole Book of Daniel
is steeped in prayer. If you have here the tumult and the shouting of the captains and the kings, you have also the deep calm
of the secret place of the Most High. Daniel himself, when death
was in the air, flung open his western windows towards Jerusalem,
and three times a day knelt praying to his fathers' God. And
Shadrach, Meshach, Abednego were men of the same breed.

Today we have lost too much the spirit of prayer. We do not
believe in it as Christ believed in it. By prayer, Jesus routed
the demons of the desert. By prayer, the apostles shook down
the throne of Nero. By prayer, Francis and Luther and Wesley
and many another brought from the four winds the breath of
God to breathe upon the dry bones of an effete ecclesiastical
institution, and the dead bones sprang to life, an exceeding great
army. By real, concentrated, believing prayer the Church today
could change the present dangerous situation out of recognition.
The real malady of the Church is not theological stagnation nor
social indifference: it is prayer paralysis.

All through this story of Daniel you can feel the waft of the
supernatural, just because these men were men of prayer. And
for ourselves, so apt to get rushed and tired and hectic and
despondent, this is the secret—the peace and poise and power of
prayer. This can still beat all the Nebuchadnezzars of life, as in
the days of old. God can deliver me out of thy clutches, O
world, and He will deliver me; but if not, if darkest tragedy and
chaos come and what men call disaster, nevertheless, O world, I
have fought the fight, I have finished the course, I have kept

the faith! 'Men,' said Jesus, 'ought always to pray, and not to faint.'

Providence and Prayer. And the final secret? The Presence: the unseen presence, that great and wonderful companionship. This was what even pagan, secular Nebuchadnezzar and his courtiers came to see. For when Shadrach, Meshach and Abednego had been flung into the furnace, not having been delivered, when all the people had been summoned to witness the execution and to deride the last agonies of that faithful remnant of a Church, suddenly they were startled by a shout: 'Look,' cried the king, with mounting terror in his voice, 'did we not cast three men into the furnace? Why are there four? And why is the fourth like a Son of God?'

We know the answer to that question, which the watchers on the plains of Babylon could not know. Who shall separate us from Christ? Not the furnace of life, nor the savagery of death; not chaos nor ruin nor a world in flames. 'When thou passest through the waters, I will be with thee; when thou walkest through the fire, the flame shall not kindle upon thee.' So that, in Charles Wesley's great words, we too can say:

> We have through fire and water gone,
> But saw Thee on the floods appear,
> But felt Thee present in the flame,
> And shouted our Deliverer's name!

Deliverance in the day of trial? Yes, please God. Yes, if it is the Father's will. But if not! If the Father should will otherwise, what then? Then—'though I walk through the valley of the shadow of death, I will fear no evil: for Thou art with me'.

It was told that when Savonarola was being marched to his death, the watching crowd saw that the martyr was repeating something over and again to himself, and those who were nearest heard what the words were. 'They may kill me if they choose —but they will never, never tear the living Christ from my heart!' This is the victory.

> Safe though all safety's lost; safe where men fall;
> And if these poor limbs die, safest of all.

V

WHEN CHRIST BREAKS THROUGH

'Thomas said ... Let us also go, that we may die with Him'—John 11:16.

'Thomas saith ... Lord, we know not whither Thou goest; and how can we know the way?'—John 14:5.

'But Thomas ... was not with them when Jesus came'—John 20:24.

'Thomas ... said ... My Lord and my God'—John 20:28.

It is a tremendous thing to see a good man's faith rising out of the depths and storming the heights. That is what we are going to see now; and the dramatic thing about it is that it is not an old story at all, but absolutely contemporary.

This disciple Thomas has never had justice done to him by posterity. He has been a man anathematised by a label, branded by an epithet—Thomas the doubter, the sceptic, the agnostic. I submit that this is monstrously unfair. Let me recall to you briefly the four scenes in which he plays a part.

Scene One. This is away beyond the Jordan to the north-east. It was at a time when Jesus and His friends had barely escaped with their lives from the murderous hatred of Jerusalem. Now in their quiet retreat they were having a blessed week of untroubled and refreshing peace.

Then suddenly one day there came a message from near Jerusalem, from the home of Mary and Martha in Bethany, an urgent message to say that their brother Lazarus was dying. And they all wondered nervously what Jesus would do. 'Come,' He said at last, 'we are needed, let us go.' Whereupon they burst into protest—all of them except one. 'But Master,' they cried, 'it's madness! To go anywhere near Judaea, now that the whole Jerusalem Establishment have their knife in you, is running into the very jaws of destruction. It is courting certain death!' So they protested, until it looked as if there would be a mutiny, and Jesus would be left to take the dangerous road alone. Then one quiet voice spoke up: 'Let us also go, that we may die with Him.' That was Thomas, courageous, loyal Thomas, putting even Peter and John to shame. Somehow that quiet word settled the matter, so that all twelve of them rose and followed their Master, on towards the thunderladen menace of Jerusalem.

In the light of an incident like that, do you not feel that Thomas has scarcely had justice done to him? Whatever else you say about him, don't dare to call him pusillanimous. His true place is with the bravest of the brave.

The annals of the thirteenth century tell of Simon de Montfort, founder of Parliament, who died at the battle of Evesham for the civil liberties of the land. The night before the battle, he had a premonition of his death, and told it to those around him. But one of his men, Hugh Despenser, expressed with the simplicity of unqualified devotion the feelings of them all. 'If you die,' he exclaimed, 'we have no wish to live.' And when next day the descending darkness stilled the noise of battle where de Montfort lay slain, his followers, true to their word, lay all around him, loyal in life and death.

'If you die, we have no wish to live.' That was the authentic Thomas spirit. It is like the great cry of Tolstoy in his story *Resurrection*, 'Why should my friend die, and I be left alive?' That calls to mind, back in the Old Testament, in the Book of Samuel, the magnificent words of one rough soldier who served under David: 'Wherever my lord the king shall be, whether in death or life, even there also shall thy servant be!'

That is the Thomas spirit exactly. 'Are my Master's fortunes ruined?' he thought. 'Death staring Him in the face? No one to stand beside Him now? All the more reason why I should be there. Let us also go, that we may die with Him.' George Whitefield, that mighty preacher, once broke out startlingly with this— 'If I am going to be damned, at least it will be at the feet of Jesus!'

I ask you, how dare we look down on this man, tagging on a damaging epithet to his name—sceptic, agnostic, heretic—and sending him down the years with that? No. Here was a man who,

looking into the eyes of his Master, could say to Jesus such
words as a poet says to his beloved:

> I will not let thee go.
> The stars that crowd the summer skies
> Have watched us so below
> With all their million eyes,
> I dare not let thee go.
>
> I will not let thee go.
> I hold thee by too many bands:
> Thou sayest farewell, and lo!
> I have thee by the hands,
> And will not let thee go.

So we shall have to revise our estimate. About his loyalty there
can be no question.

What then? Whence came his difficulty? It came, as I believe
the narrative makes clear, from the very sensitivity of his nature.
The penalty of a sensitive nature is that sometimes it may land
you in moods of fatalism and pessimism and depression. This
is the particular private devil against which many a sensitive
spirit has to fight.

Does that not come out even in those brave words of Thomas?
'Let us also go, that we may die with Him.' You see? The
darkest possible reading of the situation, the instinctive assump-
tion that the worst was bound to happen: 'The cause is ruined
anyway—we might as well go down with it together.'

Who is going to cast the first stone at Thomas for that? Have
we never, facing the daunting facts of our contemporary situation—the violence, the moral chaos, the distorted scales of values,
the generation gap, the racial tensions, the stark ferocious poverty
of two-thirds of the human race, the endemic crisis of international politics, problems shouting at us from every newspaper's
headlines, every television screen—have we never felt that here
is something beyond any power on earth to solve? No, it is not
an old story: it is utterly contemporary.

So we pass to the next place where Thomas plays a part.
Scene Two. This was a couple of weeks later. It was in the upper

room in Jerusalem. Jesus was speaking the shining, incomparable words that have lit a lamp of hope for multitudes. 'Let not your heart be troubled. You believe in God—believe also in Me. In My Father's house are many mansions. I go to prepare a place for you. And where I go you know, and the way you know.' It was at that point that Thomas suddenly broke in and interrupted. 'Lord,' he blurted out, 'we don't know where you are going—and how can we know the way?'

That was not defiant scepticism or callow rationalism or anything of the kind. It was the reaction of a sensitive spirit to the deepening crisis of the hour. 'Let not your heart be troubled.' 'Yes,' cried the heart of Thomas, 'but with dreams broken, plans wrecked, and hopes blacked out, how can we help being troubled?' 'In My Father's house are many mansions.' 'Yes, but what if it was a kingdom here and now we looked for, not far ethereal mansions in the skies?' 'Whither I go you know.' 'But, Lord, we don't know, for the sun is gone from our sky, and night and darkness rushing up, and we can't see the way. Why mock us by speaking riddles? Master, it is not kind!'

Surely you will be gentle to this man with that mood upon him: for those black hours of sultry weather in the soul—do we not know them ourselves? Days when we ask ourselves— What is the world coming to? Is there any way through the labyrinth ahead? Nineteen centuries of Christianity—are we any nearer the New Jerusalem yet? If Christ is Lord of history, where is He leading us? We certainly can't see the way—with this earth a chaos and a shambles still, morally, spiritually, internationally. 'We enter church,' complained Thomas Hardy, 'and have to sing "My soul doth magnify the Lord", when what we want to sing is, "O that my soul could find some Lord that it could magnify!"' It is difficult then not to fall victim to the Omar Khayyam mood:

> Ah, Love! Could thou and I with fate conspire
> To grasp this sorry Scheme of Things entire,
>   Would not we shatter it to bits—and then
> Remould it nearer to the Heart's Desire?

But wait! As poetry, that may be splendid; as a philosophy of life, it is ruinous. 'It is a great thing,' said R. L. Stevenson, 'to believe in immortality: but first of all it is necessary to believe in life.' Is it not one of Christ's tremendous achievements, that He has helped so many souls at the breaking-point to do precisely that—to believe in life, to cease the disenchanted dirge about this 'sorry scheme of things', and to stand up on their feet before the face of God and praise Him for His grace?

And if today our worship here could connect up even one besieged, beleaguered soul with that dimension of eternity, and could touch one such life with the penetrating, permeating power of the Spirit, this service would certainly not have been in vain. I do know this: whoever you are, whatever the circumstances, Christ can make you a conquering personality. He can break the deadlock, and put on to your very face from this moment the dignity of the peace of God which passes understanding.

Mark you, to say that is not to turn away into a little private spiritual haven, or to minimise the world's ferocious woes and troubles—God forbid! It is to involve you in this troubled world more deeply, more sacrificially than ever; but at the same time to reinforce you with the spirit of One who in the blackest night saw, luminous beyond the shadows, the undefeatable sovereignty of God, and gives you this authoritative word today—'Be of good cheer, I have overcome the world.'

Come back, then, to Thomas. *Scene Three.* This is a scene where Thomas ought to have played a part, but did not. It was now Easter evening. The gloaming was gathering on that greatest day that ever was from the foundation of the world. There in Jerusalem behind barred and bolted doors the little group was waiting—not twelve now, not eleven, just ten—waiting in the twilight for something to happen, they scarcely knew what. Meanwhile they were praying. They were on their knees. 'Lord, have mercy upon us! Christ, have mercy upon us. Lord, have mercy upon us.' Then, in a moment, it happened—the sense of a Presence, the darkness flooded with a sudden light, the music of a dear remembered voice: 'Peace be unto you.' And now, their fears of the Jews all flung to the winds, 'Hail, Master,' they were crying, 'Lord Jesus, hail!' But, adds the evangelist laconically, 'Thomas was not with them when Jesus came.'

I want you to think of that. Two of the disciples, only two, were missing that night, Judas and Thomas. We know why Judas was not there: the field of blood could tell that. But Thomas—where was he? The writer of the letter to the Hebrews says, 'Forsake not the assembling of yourselves together, as the manner of some is.' Don't fail to stand with your fellow-Christians when they meet to wait on the Lord, adoring God's goodness and asking for His mercy and giving Him their love. Here was a man who missed Christ by not being in church when He came. And Christ missed Thomas. You may be sure of that. Christ noticed the empty place. Let us remember this, when we absent ourselves too lightly or thoughtlessly from the worshipping fellowship, or when perhaps there are burdens on our spirit that keep us apart and aloof, disinclined to join in the prayers and praises of the sanctuary. Why was the place empty? 'Thomas was not with them'—what can have kept him away?

Was he feeling too preoccupied that night to go to church? Was the road too long, the wind too cold, his own fireside too comfortable? No, not that—he had no fireside of his own to sit at. Why, then, was he not there? Was he tired of the sound of Peter's voice, bored with the ritual of religion, afraid he might be asked to lead in prayer, telling himself that in any case nothing would happen? Was it with Thomas as sometimes it is with us —we are not in the mood, and so we stay away?

But think what he lost! In the middle of that church service came Jesus. And 'Thomas was not with them when Jesus came'. He missed that. And that coming of Jesus always happens. It is this that makes every ordinary worship gathering—drab and humdrum and all too vitiated by human ineptitudes as it may seem—essentially supernatural and miraculous. 'Where two or three are gathered in My name, there am I in the midst of them.' Thomas isolated himself from that.

But I do not think we have found the deepest reason for his absence yet. I think that Thomas that night was walking some dark deserted road of Jerusalem, alone with his griefs and his memories. I see him wandering aimlessly, hardly knowing what way he was taking, and then finding with a start that his steps had led him out to Golgotha. He climbed the slope to the brow of the hill, and there, dim against the night sky, were the three crosses still, gaunt and empty now; and everything deadly quiet, where so recently there had been the tramp of soldiers, and the shouts of the multitude, and the weeping of women—eerily still and quiet now, only the night wind rustling the treetops, and perhaps far off the baying of some beast of prey prowling in the ravines of the valley. And there, all alone, this loving loyal soul fell on his knees at one of the crosses, and clasped the cold timber of it with his arms. There was the mark of the blood still! Let us leave him with his thoughts—this man like Sir Bedivere at the passing of Arthur, revolving many memories and crying, in the stillness of the dead world's winter dawn, 'the King is gone!'

The King was gone. But next morning, back in Jerusalem, passing down a familiar street, Thomas was accosted. It was Peter and John, hurrying along, with a strange light on their faces. 'Man,' they cried, 'where have you been? Why were you not with us? We have seen the Lord!' But their mood just exasperated him. What right had they to be so excited at a time like this? 'You are dreaming and deluded,' he told them. 'It is just some crazy story put about by Mary Magdalene. I shan't be any party to it. I'd have to grasp and hold Him, before I would believe!'

We can understand that outburst. It is not intellectual difficulties that breed such moods, not the cold breath of rational scepticism that does the damage: it is the strain of life, the stormy gust of the whirlwind of trouble—it is this that blows out the lights and leaves the soul in darkness.

But what is Christ's gospel but the assurance of a way by which any man, any woman, can rise in the strength of God and sweep the midnight from the soul?

So we come to the last act now. *Scene Four.* It was seven days since that first Easter night. What a week that had been for Thomas—the loneliness of it, the heartache, the bitter crushing hopelessness! Until one day at last Peter and John sought him out. 'Tomorrow,' they told him, 'we are gathering in the upper room again. Tomorrow again we are expecting Jesus to come. Will you join us this time? Come, friend, we specially want you to be there!' 'Why should I?' he retorted. 'Must you go on unloading your delusions upon me? Why keep reopening the wound?' But that night he could not sleep. He kept wondering uneasily. Peter and John had seemed so manifestly convinced. 'What if they should be right, and I am wrong? What if their tale is true, and I am the stubborn blunderer?' There in the dark lonely hours of the night his mind was made up. He would join the others on the morrow.

So again it was the first day of the week, and again the disciples were at prayer in the upper room, and this time Thomas with them. I can hear Peter's voice leading them in their devotions. 'O Jesus, risen and alive, come to us today! Dear Master, Conqueror of death, hear our prayer, and let our cry come unto Thee. Show Thyself to our brother here, that he may share our gladness!' And then the answer, sudden, overwhelming. This strange, luminous Presence! That familiar voice! Had time rolled back, thought Thomas, and Calvary never happened? Or was it, could it be, the King alive from the dead? All at once he knew it. He knew it so certainly that he never waited even to apply the test which the Saviour Himself had proposed, the test of reaching out to touch the wounded hands and side. 'Jesus, Master, it was true after all—my Lord and my God!'

Surely it means something tremendously important—that the finest confession of faith in the whole New Testament comes from Thomas! Not one of them—Peter, John, Matthew—could comprise the essence of the faith in more forthright unequivocal words. My Lord and my God.

What does it mean for us? It means this—that the most perplexed and troubled soul in this church today can, by the grace of God, come right out of that uncertainty and be the most exultant Christian of us all.

Do you believe this thing I am telling you? You see, it is not our poor faltering search for Christ that really matters: that is a mere fraction of what religion is about. The basic fact of life is this—that God in Christ is for ever seeking us. And that being so, it follows that here in this church today we are actually standing on the frontiers of the unseen world.

Jesus had indeed marked Thomas's absence on the earlier occasion. He always does. He knows why one or another has forsaken the assembly of God's people. And this time He singled Thomas out, giving him a personal message individually addressed, and in amazing generosity adapting His revelation to the man's particular need. That is Jesus' way.

And the same Christ who did this for Thomas is here today to do it for someone else: to come right across that frontier of the world unseen, to break through the closed door in loving-kindness and tender mercy and scatter the midnight of the soul. This thing is true. He is coming over the horizon of someone now, the eternal Christ, the Spirit of life and light and love. Lift up your heart to the dawn that is breaking. Jesus, my Lord and my God!

VI

RUMOUR OR REALITY?

'Then the Lord answered Job out of the whirlwind and said, Who is this that darkeneth counsel by words without knowledge? Gird up now thy loins like a man; for I will demand of thee, and answer thou Me ... Then Job answered the Lord, and said ... I have heard of Thee by the hearing of the ear: but now mine eye seeth Thee. Wherefore I abhor myself, and repent in dust and ashes'—Job 38:1-3; 42:1, 5, 6.

'I have heard of Thee by the hearing of the ear.' Well, that is something at any rate. Not much of a creed perhaps, but at least better than nothing: hardly a trumpet-toned confession, but always a beginning.

In one sense, of course, hardly anyone goes through this world without hearing of God by the hearing of the ear. Even our sceptics and agnostics and secularist critics have at least heard of Him. And as for most of us in this church today, we have heard of God from our earliest days and our mothers' arms. One Name above all glorious names has thrust itself upon us, all down the journey of the years. 'Have you not known,' cries Isaiah, 'have you not heard? Has it not been told you from the beginning, from the foundations of the earth?'

But now observe—this is very important—the period of Job's life to which these words apply. 'I have heard of Thee'—that was in his prosperous, untroubled days. That was when everything was stable and normal and secure. He was then the typical, decent, well-to-do citizen, accepting his privileged social status as a right. Religious? Oh yes, he was religious. In fact, he could be quite eloquent about that, with a warm glow of sentiment at the thought of his religion and what it meant to him. Not that it would ever have occurred to him in those days to call himself a 'miserable sinner'. He was not miserable, and he did not feel much of a sinner. Those Chaldeans over the border, they were sinners all right—those beastly brigands always indulging in border raids and thieving their neighbours' cattle—miserable sinners indeed: but for himself, his life and character were satis-factory enough. That was Job as he had been once upon a time. That was the period of his life of which, looking back now, he says 'I had heard of Thee, Lord, with the hearing of the ear.'

Now let us pause there for a moment. For this is where a good many of us who profess and call ourselves Christians stand today. 'I have heard of Thee.' So often it stops at hearsay. In fact, we rather like to have it that way—inherited, or traditional, or con-ventional, rather than real and alive and experimental. We believe in God coolly and objectively, but not with any kind of breath-less gratitude, not with the desperate passionate intentness of the man who cried—'My soul thirsts for God, for the living God. When shall I come and appear before God?'

'I had heard of Thee by the hearing of the ear.' It is the difference between studying the map of a country and actually living in the country itself. You can be quite a connoisseur in maps, without once setting foot abroad. You can know a lot of theology, and yet be detached and non-committal as to the divine reality.

I am not decrying maps—nothing so foolish. They tabulate what others have discovered; they are necessary for anyone who is to go travelling. I am not minimising the theology which is the map of the Kingdom of God: it tabulates what generations of Christians have found, and it is necessary for anyone who would be a pilgrim. But surely the important thing is not to know all about the map: it is to get into the country ourselves. Why should we, why should anyone, stop short at—'I had heard of Thee with the hearing of the ear'? It is so stale and sterile, that religion!

Job did not stop there. Suddenly he adds—'But now—now mine eye seeth Thee!' What had come in between? What had turned hearsay into direct encounter?

Two things: an experience and a revelation. An experience of life in the depths, and a revelation of God in the heights: two events—which were really not two, but one. In actual fact, they interlocked and interpenetrated each other indissolubly. But it will help us to clarify what happened if for the moment we view them apart.

First, the experience. It is there in the early chapters of the book: this man's experience of trouble, dreadful, heartbreaking trouble. And mark this well: it was not only his health and his home and his happiness that had crashed in one all-engulfing cataclysm—though that was true. But something else as well had gone with the wind of that frightful hurricane: his philosophy of life, his conventional code which had never faced up to the depth and tragedy of existence, his conscious rectitude and religiosity—that too had crashed in ruin. And the man looked up from the wreckage. 'I had heard of Thee with the hearing of the ear; but now—now out of the depths—mine eye seeth Thee!'

Now we all know there are many different ways of encountering God. Other men have met God along quite different roads—Wordsworth in nature, Haydn in music, Teilhard de Chardin in science, and so on. But here is one of the classic ways—the way of trouble, the way of the wind and the whirlwind. When a man faces the night and the tempest; when civilisation finds the old secure foundations shaking and tottering beneath it; when a nation looks out over a final abyss, as we did after Dunkirk, or as all the nations do today, poised on the precipice of this nuclear age; when the great inexorable questions about the meaning of life and the purpose of it all hit our souls like a tornado—it can be then, in the mercy of providence, that the hour of vision comes.

John Bunyan was thrown into prison. It was a terrible experience. But listen! 'Never in all my life,' he declared, 'have I had so great an inlet into the Word of God as now. Those Scriptures that I saw nothing in before have begun in this place to shine upon me.' The Covenanters, hunted and harried over the moors, declared that never had they experienced such fellowship with Christ as when the enemy dragoons were after them. 'I was not persuaded into religion,' wrote Cowper the poet, 'I was scourged into it'—not persuaded, scourged. And anything that crashes violently through the defences of our common days can be a potential preparation for a new coming of the Lord. 'I had heard,' said Job, 'in my secure untroubled days that now seem so fantastically remote, I had heard of Thee with the hearing of the ear; but now—in the devastating experience that has torn up my life and battered my defences—now mine eye seeth Thee!'

I am not saying, mark you, that trouble always has this effect. That would not be honest. Trouble does not automatically sanctify. Sometimes it does the opposite. Sometimes it breeds not saints but cynics. Sometimes it does not soften the spirit, but makes it hard and bitter. The fact is, trouble in itself is neutral. It needs something else—it needs the Spirit of God—to make it not neutral but positive and creative. Listen to one who had found this great secret. 'It doesn't matter,' wrote Hudson Taylor of China, 'how great the pressure is; it only matters where the pressure lies—whether it comes between you and God, or whether it presses you near and ever nearer to His heart of love.' That is the great question. Is the pressure of life to thrust you into unbelief and denial—or to thrust you into the arms of the eternal?

So we come back to Job. I have said there were two things that turned his hearsay, second-hand religion into direct, first-hand encounter—two events that were really not two, but one. There was experience—we have seen that now, the experience of life in the depths. Along with that, there was revelation, the revelation of God in the heights.

Job, of course, had no vision of Christ, such as we have to help us through the dark places. But he did have a revelation of another kind.

It was indeed an overpowering revelation. You must read again those magnificent closing chapters of the book, where God speaks out of the whirlwind, that colossal cataract of questions from the mouth of the Almighty. 'Who is this that darkeneth counsel by words without knowledge? Gird up thy loins like a man, and answer Me!' Do read it: it is so relevant today when there are voices, influential confident voices, telling us that man's cosmic achievements have dethroned the God of the Bible, so that we are now free to start playing at being little gods for ourselves. What crazed and fatuous nonsense! Here, to demolish it, is this torrent of questions from the mouth of the Almighty, rapid, relentless, resistless—more than one hundred and twenty verses of them: 'Where wast thou when I laid the foundations of the earth? Hast thou commanded the morning forth? Canst thou bind the Pleiades or loose the bands of Orion? Canst thou play with the stars? Hast thou an arm like God?'—and so the torrent of questions rolls on and on, till you almost expect to hear Job shouting, 'O God, that's enough! Have mercy. Stop before You bludgeon me unconscious!'

But now, look! What was actually happening was this—that under the hammering of those questions something that had been hard and frozen in Job's heart was melting. Under the self-disclosure of God Almighty, he was beginning to see himself as he truly was: to see, in the light of the overwhelming power of the eternal his own powerlessness, in the light of the infinite wisdom his own infantile pretensions, in the light of that blazing holiness his own smudged radical corruption. 'Now mine eye seeth Thee. Wherefore I abhor myself, and repent in dust and ashes.'

How does it strike you, that revulsion and self-abhorring? Is it just the nauseating piety of a grovelling self-depreciation? That is certainly what our Freudian friends would call it. Most of us do not take kindly to Job's language, do we? We shrug it off with the word 'morbid'. We say to the poor preacher, 'Why in all the world choose a text like that? Couldn't the man have found something more cheerful in the Bible to talk about?'

No, it is not congenial to the modern mood. It is not considered appropriate to man's maturity and mastery of nature in this technologically sophisticated age. The modern mood is to say—'What a wonderful architect of destiny man is! What a brave new world he is fashioning! What a marvellous Utopia he is heading for!'

Yes, perhaps. I am not minimising any of this twentieth century's colossal achievements. One would have to be an ungrateful fool to do that. What I do have to say is this: that unless I have stood where Job stood when he bowed his head and cried 'I abhor myself, I am stripped of everything; nothing in my hands I bring', unless I have been there, I have never begun to grasp what Christ's religion is all about—dying in order to live—and certainly I have never reached the point where my human personality can have its conventional crust broken up, and be ready to receive at the depths of its being the seal and impression of God.

'I repent in dust and ashes', declared Job. Suppose we ask: what does that word repent mean today, in the light of the Christian revelation? It means change direction, reorientate my life, face resolutely the fact of my human impotence to be my own redeemer—and then turn right round and *face Jesus Christ*, with all the windows of my being flung wide open to the inrush of His triumphant power.

It is all focused in these two words: face Christ. We have seen how God confronted Job in an experience of darkness, and in a sudden flash of revelation. Today for us it is the same, yet gloriously different.

God confronts us in the darkest hour of terrible trouble that ever entered history: we call it now Good Friday. God meets us in a place of darkness such as was never seen nor known since time began nor ever again shall be. He meets us at the cross, the place where Jesus takes all the troubles of the world upon Himself. There in that death of violence and glory, in that fierce whirlwind hour of cruelty and passion; there, not sitting remote and aloof in some high untroubled heaven, but down in the ferocious shambles of this tragic earth, which still today is so full of muddle and misery, violence and devilry; there on the eternal gibbet of history—God meets us there. Out of the whirlwind the Almighty answers, the whirlwind of Calvary. And what can I say but this? 'I had heard of Thee with the hearing of the ear: but now—now at the cross—mine eye seeth Thee!' And if that means dust and ashes, as it does, it certainly does not leave me there; for this is the vision of God that gives beauty for ashes, joy for mourning, so that the dirge of self-abhorrence changes into the shouts and hallelujahs of the redeemed.

Let me, in closing, make this quite personal. Today someone has a heavy burden. I plead with you: do look out beyond yourself to the great burden-bearer of humanity!

Surely you must believe it—that if out of that terrible trouble of Calvary the eternal love brought victoriously the salvation of the world, it is not beyond its power to bring something positive and shining and creative out of your trouble.

This is the logic of the gospel. It is not in any sense an emotional appeal. It is an appeal by the strict logic and rationality of faith.

The question is this. Do you think it likely that, having died on the cross for love of you, He would then refuse the minor gift you are needing now? That having given His life, He would then refuse a cup of cold water?

I do not know the particular private problem that may be tormenting the soul of someone here today, nor what secret sorrows may be present. I do not know what the darkness of the future hides. I only know that Christ, who died for love of you, has given His promise and is quite certain to be there. I only know that, because He is there, you can see the dark hour through and lead captivity captive. I only know you can face the wind and the whirlwind by His reinforcing grace.

And I pray it may be one result of this hour of worship that someone who came in here weary and heavy-laden may go out with spirit made strong and calm in the ineffable serenity of Jesus.

> I fear no foe, with Thee at hand to bless;
> Ills have no weight, and tears no bitterness ...
> I triumph still if Thou abide with me.

Do you remember how Bunyan's pilgrim, at the beginning of his journey, met Evangelist and asked him for directions about the way? Evangelist pointed into the distance, and said 'Do you see yonder wicket-gate?' Christian looked, and looked again, and had to answer 'No.' Then said Evangelist, 'Do you see yonder shining light?'—almost as though to say 'Do you see one spot where the darkness is not quite so dark as all the rest?' And Christian gazed, shading his eyes with his hand, and then answered—'I think I do.' Then said Evangelist, 'Keep that light in your eye. That is the way for you!'

Today it is not always easy to see the gate—the gateway that leads through to a truly authentic existence and to fullness of life. There is so much that is perplexing and difficult to understand, perhaps doctrines and dogmas of the Church that leave you cold. But today, I offer you Christ—the only thing, after all, the Church exists to do—and I ask: Do you see yon shining light? Or at least, do you see one spot in the darkness where the darkness is not quite so dark as all the rest? And if you say, 'Yes, I think I do,' then that is salvation. That is everything you need. 'I had heard of You, O God, with the hearing of the ear; but now, in the face of Jesus, my eye sees You, luminous against the darkness of the world.'

That is the way for me, for you, for all mankind. Do believe this thing I am telling you. Do act upon it. And God bless you, pilgrim soul, upon the way.

> And in that light of life you'll walk
> Till travelling days are done.

VII

JESUS AND THE HEREAFTER

'They confessed that they were strangers and pilgrims on the earth ...
God is not ashamed to be called their God; for He hath prepared for
them a city'—Hebrews 11:13, 16.

We are being constantly told that Christianity today has to
face what is called 'the problem of communication'. It must speak
in an idiom understood by the modern mind. It must reckon with
the modern mood. It must preach a gospel relevant to the contemporary situation. This is obviously very important.

But now if the question be asked, What is the prevailing
modern mood? the answer is clear. It is a spirit of this-worldliness. Where an earlier age riveted its gaze on the life beyond, this
age is predominantly concerned with the here and now.

Let us by all means give this mood its due. At its best, it is an
entirely right emphasis, with nothing discreditable about it. The
very reverse! It represents a Christ-created social passion, a true
concern for the conditions in which men and women have to live
here on earth. To regard existence here as merely an unimportant
prelude to something more significant to follow would surely be
to do scant justice to life's true values. No one indeed can doubt
the importance of the here and now who has begun to understand
the meaning of the Incarnation, when the Word was made flesh.
Christianity, when true to its Master, will never disdain the
material, secular world. In this sense, the modern this-worldliness,
the emphasis on the here and now, is deeply and truly religious.
If we do not find God in the duties and relationships of the
common day, it is not likely we shall find Him at all.

So we are living in a generation that has reacted strongly
against any beguiling pietistic otherworldliness. The world is
rightly intolerant—sometimes fiercely and furiously intolerant—
of any religion that counsels acquiescence in the face of remedi-

able evils. As Dr. A. C. Craig, that fine interpreter of the faith, expressed it vividly and forcibly in his Warrack Lectures: 'There must be something farcical and fraudulent in the kind of pietism which preaches from villas in the West End to slums in the East End about mansions in heaven.' That is well and truly said.

But now, I wonder—is it possible that the pendulum may swing too far? There are indications that something of this kind has been happening. One such indication is the vogue of a belief in inevitable progress on the horizontal level, as our scientific and technological civilisation marches on. You get a kind of apotheosis of humanist activism and secular Utopianism. Man, by his own efforts, is destined to create an earthly paradise, and he needs no other home.

But what is more surprising and disquieting is this—that the swing of the pendulum away from otherworldliness can be discerned, not only in society and culture generally, but also in the Church. We may be pilgrims and sojourners, as all our fathers were; we may repeat that 'here we have no continuing city'; but we contrive with a fair degree of success to forget it. We make this bivouac of earth our home. We fortify our brief encampment with the ramparts of material security. We are earthbound, and proud of it. The shouting and the tumult of the planners and the organisers drown the voice that cries from heaven, 'This is not your rest!—no abiding city.' This, I repeat, is true even of Christian people, even of the Church.

May it be that our understandable anxiety to plead 'Not guilty' to the accusation of anything in the nature of escapism and pietism has led to the soft-pedalling of some of the faith's characteristic notes? Sometimes indeed one gets the impression that Christians are almost falling over backwards in their eagerness to dissociate themselves from the 'pilgrims and sojourners' conception of the New Testament—in case they should even be suspected of the false otherworldliness at which Marx and Nietzsche in a former generation and Russell and Ayer today have launched their anathemas. Sometimes institutional Christianity has been so bent upon refuting the charge of making religion a tranquilliser, an opiate, so eager to prove its passionate involvement in the life of the here and now, and specially in every crusade against glaring social injustices, that it has been almost afraid to talk of the hereafter at all. So the characteristic trumpet-note of Christian assurance gets blurred and muffled.

Yet the fact remains that the problem of the hereafter haunts, and will always haunt, the mind of man. The concentration on the here and now to the exclusion of what lies beyond is an adolescent immature theology which can hardly survive any serious contemplation of the profound mysteries of the human lot, in which suffering and evil and an appalling sense of transitoriness are inextricably interwoven with the very pattern of existence. This is written plainly all over the Bible. 'Man goeth to his long home, and the mourners go about the streets. The silver cord is loosed, the golden bowl is broken, the pitcher is broken at the fountain, the wheel broken at the cistern.' 'All flesh is grass, and all the goodliness thereof is at the flower of the field. The grass withereth, the flower fadeth.' 'The beauty of Israel is slain upon thy high places. Thy love to me was wonderful, passing the love of women. How are the mighty fallen, and the weapons of war perished!' In scores of such magnificent resounding passages the Bible makes it plain that if man is haunted by the question of the hereafter it is because he is haunted by the fact of death.

This is a truth—to turn for a moment to the realm of music— that has been expressed in one of the world's great symphonies. It was the symphony composed by Tchaikovsky in the last months of his life and conducted by him just a week before his death, the great B minor Symphony, full of questioning and agitation, with the exciting, overwhelming rhythms of the march in the penultimate movement giving way to the tragic desolation of the last. 'The haunting of life by death'—this was Tchaikovsky's own description of his theme. And certainly the music conveys it. Incidentally, over against this music of Tchaikovsky one might well set, by way of complete contrast, Brahms' *Requiem*. Here death is still the theme, but pessimism there is none, and always the sombre mood merges into the great fortifying climaxes of victory and peace.

But now to return. I want you to observe that there are three specific ways in which death haunts the mind of man.

It haunts him as he looks at history. What about the countless generations over which the waves of time have gone? There *a.* was a day when Xerxes, king of Persia, reviewing his mighty host marching against Greece, broke down and wept: he wept to think that in a hundred years not one of them would be left. 'Thou carriest them away as with a flood.' Have all these myriad multitudes just vanished, and ceased to be?

But it haunts man more personally as he meditates on his own experience. To the child or to the youth unlimited time *b.* seems to stretch away before him, incalculable prospects to beckon him on his way. But by the age of forty, if not much earlier, time is recognised as a rapidly dwindling possession, 'a watch in the night': so many of the noble prospects that ambition once proposed are pitifully restricted, and out of the shadows comes the question 'Why have I to go down the hill into the westering sunset, and die before half my work is done?'

Above all, it haunts man in the region of his love. It may be possible, through the wisdom born of advancing years, to view *C.* with equanimity the ending of our own brief day; it is not possible to be indifferent to the severance of earth's most precious ties when death invades the circle of our love.

> Till a' the seas gang dry, my dear,
>   And the rocks melt wi' the sun;
> And I will love thee still, my dear,
>   While the sands o' life shall run.

Notice, further, that there is a sense in which death specially haunts the Christian. The Bible refuses to insult our intelligence by playing down death, or to outrage our feelings by soft-pedalling its element of tragedy, its fierce effrontery. It insists on reminding us that death is a major fact, an intruder in God's creation, the ultimate contradiction, 'man's last enemy'.

But now, to come to the answer. We know that all down the centuries men have been grappling with this fact—Greek *3* tragedians, Hebrew prophets, poets, philosophers, spiritualists, stoics. But what concerns us today is not that, important as it *The* may be. What concerns us is the one way above all others in *Christian Solution: Assurance of the Hereafter*

which men have seen the haunting face of death transformed and
the question of the hereafter resolved. No philosophic argument
this, but the contemplation of a fact; no analysis of fears and
hopes, no balancing of probabilities, but the rock-like firmness of
an event, the Christ-event, God's final revelation of Himself in
Jesus Christ His Son, incarnate, crucified and risen from the
dead.

It is quite certain that it was the contemplation of the fact of
Christ that gave the first Christians their assurance of the hereafter. It is vitally important to observe how this comes about.
Suppose we take some different aspects of the Christ-event. Just
see how every one of them is prophetic of the hereafter and
vibrant with the eternal hope.

Take, first, the teaching of Jesus. Here is one passage in particular. The Sadducees, you remember, did not believe in the
resurrection of the dead; and on one occasion, with the aid of
an elaborate account of seven brothers who had each married
the same woman in turn, they were endeavouring to pour scorn
on the belief. 'Whose wife shall she be in the resurrection?'
Jesus made short work of their fantastic tale; and then went on
to outflank their subtle strategy with a greater and a nobler story,
that of the burning bush, and how God had called to Moses out
of the fire and said, 'I am the God of Abraham and of Isaac and
of Jacob.' Why that name? Jesus' own comment was this: 'He
is not the God of the dead but of the living.' That meant, These
men, Abraham, Isaac, Jacob, are really alive. Their continued
existence is no fiction. For a life, any life, once united with
God by faith, and thus joined to the immortality of God, is a
life over which death has no power. This stands in Scripture
with the immeasurable authority of Christ behind it. And you
and I may well ask, What are all our unanswered questions compared with Christ's unanswerable certainty? We may well, with
Martin Luther, turn the familiar lament, 'In the midst of life we
are in death', into the glorious affirmation, 'In the midst of death
we are in life'. In God we live eternally.

Or turn from the teaching of Jesus to His active life and
ministry. Here the same outlook upon the hereafter is apparent.
Though living as a Man among men, He knew Himself to be
dwelling in the eternal world, and His true home was never

Nazareth or Capernaum but the bosom of the Father. To Christ, that eternal world of God's kingly rule was real and paramount. So thoroughly did it dominate His being and command His will that through His life and ministry the power and energy of that world burst redemptively into history, making an onslaught on the realm of evil, arresting and repulsing disease and death and decay. The healing miracles mark the triumph of life over death. Greater than any spoken argument for immortality is it to see this quality of life inherent in Jesus grappling with the principle of death and routing it from the field. 'In Him was life, and the life was the light of men.'

So from the teaching and the life of Jesus we turn to the Resurrection. It was on this fact, as on impregnable rock, that the early Church based its proclamation of the life eternal. Here was an event in history which at the same time transcended history, shattering the ordinary historical categories of space and time, and inaugurating a new creation. God's mighty act in raising Christ from the dead was a proof that the new age had broken in, the new era had projected itself out of eternity into time—so that in this one creative act the resurrection of all believers is implicit. Christ risen from the dead, said Paul, is 'the first-born of a great brotherhood'. He said again, 'If any man be in Christ, there is the new creation.' In other words, by union with Christ our resurrection life has already begun; and our mortality is daily being overlaid by and transfigured into the eternal life of Christ. And this points forward to the day when at last we shall be like Him, seeing Him as He is, and rejoicing in His presence for ever.

This brings us to the final aspect of the Christ-event which speaks of the hereafter. This is the gift of the Holy Spirit. When Paul describes the Holy Spirit as 'the earnest of our inheritance', he means that in this divine endowment which is the present possession of the Church and of all believers there is not only a pledge and a guarantee, but actually a foretaste, an anticipatory sample, a first instalment of the blessedness of heaven. Even here on earth, Paul knew and declared, even here and now, encompassed by mortality as they were, Christians were experiencing life in a new dimension, in the Spirit, the very life of God. Over this, death clearly had no power. Its imperishableness was inherent in its very quality. Life in the Spirit now is the earnest of our inheritance yonder.

Listen on this matter to that great Asiatic Christian now gone home to God, Dr. D. T. Niles of Ceylon. 'The resurrection that awaits us beyond physical death will be but the glorious consummation of the risen life which already we have in Christ.' 'The risen life we have already'—of D. T. Niles himself that was manifestly true: you could not know him, and not see the risen life there. And so I repeat: it is the actuality of life eternal as a present possession which constitutes the inalienable assurance of the life to come. 'The hour cometh, and now is.' Even now, like the vine injecting its life into the branch, Christ through the Spirit imparts to His members the very life of God. This is immortality. This is the life eternal.

Someone may say—'You are not describing my experience. I don't feel that my religion makes all that difference—tides of a new life running through me. What is more, I don't see other people's Christianity making all that difference: Church folk are just as perplexed, anxious and afraid as anyone else.'

Is that true? I am a poor inadequate Christian, an 'unprofitable servant' in discipleship. But at any rate I do know that Christ's love can stretch the horizons and draw me into the orbit of an eternal world. Moreover, I have known scores, hundreds of people—some still alive, some here no longer—whose lives have radiated, right here on earth, a waft of the supernatural, the dimension of an eternal world. The one thing needful is to possess Christ.

I know, of course, that the 'foolishness of preaching' is an earthen vessel to hold such treasure. After a lifetime of preaching, I am more conscious of that than ever. But my prayer is that there may be some here today who, looking to Christ and His gospel, and finding their daily horizons stretched with the perspective of the dimension of eternity, will turn to the future with a braver heart and a new ineffable serenity. Strangers and pilgrims on the earth, as all our fathers were, we have here no permanent abode, but we seek one out of sight. And Christ is the sufficient guarantee that it is no empty quest. 'God is not ashamed to be called their God; for He hath prepared for them a city.'

With that irrefragable certainty to rely on, why should anyone doubt or fear? Pilgrims and sojourners—yes: but one day— 'Come, ye blessed of My Father, inherit the Kingdom.' 'Death, where is thy sting? Grave, where is thy victory? Thanks be to God who gives us the victory through Christ.' 'Lord, now lettest Thou Thy servant depart in peace: for mine eyes have seen Thy salvation.'

VIII

SPORT OF FATE OR PLAN OF GOD?

'I am Joseph your brother, whom ye sold into Egypt. Now therefore be not grieved, nor angry with yourselves, that ye sold me hither; for God did send me before you, to preserve life ... So now it was not you that sent me hither, but God'—Genesis 45:4-5, 8.

What is your final interpretation of life? This is one of the most important questions any of us can ever be asked. What does life mean to you, on a total view of it? What is your ultimate verdict on its significance?

This fact—that a man's final interpretation of life is the most practical and crucially determining thing about him—was brought out forcibly by G. K. Chesterton at the beginning of his book called *Heretics*. 'It is foolish,' wrote Chesterton in his characteristic way, 'foolish, generally speaking, for a philosopher to set fire to another philosopher in Smithfield Market because they do not agree in their theory of the universe. That was done very frequently in the Middle Ages, and it failed altogether in its object. But,' went on Chesterton, 'there is one thing that is infinitely more absurd and unpractical than burning a man for his philosophy. This is the habit of saying that his philosophy does not matter.' That is true. Our way of looking at life can be the determining factor for thought and action, conditioning all our attitudes and decisions. What does this life, on a total view of it, really mean to you? Is it made up chiefly of chance and accident, uncontrolled disconnected circumstance, just one thing after another: in Omar Khayyam's words—

> 'Tis all a Chequer-board of Nights and Days
> Where Destiny with Men for Pieces plays?

Or can you say, looking life in the face and assessing all its changes and vicissitudes, 'So now it was not you that sent me hither, but God'?

In short, your life, my life, the world's life: a human tangle, or a divine plan—which?

Let us approach this question by way of one of the greatest stories in the world. I expect that as children many of us were fascinated by the story of Joseph, a tale as gripping and dramatic as anything in the *Arabian Nights*. But those who go back to this story in later years, who read it in the light of advancing experience, realise that there is far more here than an absorbing tale magnificently told; there are inward meanings, deep divine insights, which go right down to the very heart of our human experience in this world. All the mysteries of providence are focused in these simple-looking words: 'So now it was not you that sent me hither, but God.'

Joseph, in speaking thus to the brothers who had sold him into slavery, was looking back across the years behind him. He was seeing it all again—the childhood home where he had been the joy of Jacob and Rachel, his boyhood dreams, the envy and jealousy of his brothers, the plots to disinherit him, the dark Satanic deed that sold him to the Midianite slave-dealers, his servitude in Egypt, his gradual rise to favour and promotion at the court of Pharaoh, his solving of the nation's rationing problem in the years of famine, his appointment as Prime Minister of Egypt, Commissioner-General and First Lord of the Treasury. He was seeing it all in retrospect; and there in front of him were his brothers, the same men who at the first had so villainously and treacherously dealt with him; there they were, not recognising him now, a delegation humbly supplicating aid for famine-stricken Israel. Then comes the dramatic moment of self-disclosure: 'I am Joseph your brother, whom you sold into Egypt. But be not grieved nor angry with yourselves that you sold me hither; for God sent me before you, to preserve life. So now it was not you who sent me hither, but God.'

This is worth pondering. Here was a man who through long years of thwarting and frustration had clung doggedly to the faith that the God to whom he prayed could bring good out of evil. He had been the victim of cruel and savage injustice. We could have understood it if, in the bitterness of his soul, he had blown out the light of faith and grown soured, cynical, rebellious. But the splendid thing is this—that through all those weary years Joseph had consistently refused to surrender the belief that somewhere within the shadows a beneficent transcendent will was working, that therefore there could be no such thing as an irreparable disaster, and that the very tragedy he had suffered would be used as the raw material for a mighty purpose of good. 'What I do thou knowest not now, but thou shalt know hereafter!'

Is this just a pious fabricated fable—or can we really confront the vicissitudes of life with a faith like that? To know that, whatever happens to you in this world, your life can be not the sport of fate but a plan of God; to see the dark, sombre threads being taken by the Master's hand and woven along with the brightly coloured ones into the final pattern; to know that no grim array of harsh-featured circumstance can pluck you or your loved ones out of the great Father's care or defeat His final purpose of love; to know that things can never go so far wrong that the living God cannot control and bend them to His will, and that there are no thorns so sharp that God's fingers cannot weave them into a crown of glory—this, and this alone, is life, joy, victory and serenity.

But we must be careful to discriminate here. When Joseph said to the men who had sold him into slavery, 'It was not you who sent me hither but God,' the words do not mean that God had actually willed their treacherous deed. God is never the author of evil in that sense. Unless we get that fact clear and hold it steadily before our minds, we shall fall into hopeless confusion in our thinking about the ways of providence. Are you to say it was God's will that Joseph's cruel and cunning brothers should hatch their merciless plots against him? Was it God who suggested to them their diabolical trickery and wretched deception? If you make God the author of evil in that way, then indeed chaos is come again.

Look at it like this. We can certainly see how God used the stoning of Stephen as a divine factor for the conversion of Saul of Tarsus. That is written clear in the narrative. But it certainly does not mean that God incited the martyrdom. Nor does it in any way exculpate the men who threw the stones. Or again: the fact that John Bunyan was inspired by God to employ his imprisonment for composing the *Pilgrim's Progress* does not palliate the blatant, callous intolerance that had cast him into prison.

So here. The fact that Joseph's presence in Egypt was used by God not only to keep the people of Israel alive in famine but to prepare them for their great and glorious destiny across the centuries—that fact does not extenuate the crime that at the first had torn him from his home and sold him as a slave to the Egyptians.

What, then, are we to say? Surely this. God may indeed permit evil to darken the world: He has to accept that risk, if men are to have their freedom. But it is not God who wills the evil—that is the world, the flesh and the devil. God may indeed permit the afflictions and agonies which all of us are liable to encounter in this strange uncertain world. But to say that God directly sends these shattering experiences would be a monstrous distortion of the truth. For, as the apostle says, 'God is light, and in Him is no darkness at all.'

But now, that being so, how can Joseph here declare 'It was not you who sent me hither but God'? Was that just contradiction? Some kind of facile paradox or theological distortion? No, indeed. It was the insight of faith. To Joseph, delving down beneath the surface of life's events, there had come this deep, tremendous revelation—that even when evil has taken the game firmly into its hands, God is still master of the situation. Even when things seem to have gone tragically wrong, God can still—through men who will yield themselves to His control—use the anguish creatively, to bring out of it a new and wonderful blessing that could scarce have come any other way.

Now all this, I grant you, is a somewhat abstract generalisation; and like so many abstract generalisations, it might not be particularly helpful. But, blessed be God, the whole thing has come alive in Jesus of Nazareth. The abstract generalisation has suddenly become concrete actual event, the word has been made flesh. Surely the deepest significance of this Joseph story is that its interpretation of life is focused to a burning point of revelation in the person of the greater Joseph, in the passion and victory of Christ.

Look at it like this. Take this parallel. Joseph's brothers sold him into slavery. It was their way of being rid of him. Were Christ's brothers so very different? 'He came unto His own, and His own received Him not.' It was one of His own disciples—Judas, one of the twelve—who sold Him to death. It was His own beloved Peter who denied with oaths and curses that he knew anything about Him. All His chosen fellowship forsook Him and fled and left Him to His fate. His own people mocked and spat upon Him. The brothers of His ancestral faith handed Him over to the Gentiles, in the person of Pontius Pilate and the Romans, to have Him put out of the way for ever. His own dear city of David cast Him outside its gates to die. If ever the devil was active in history, it was in the forces that planned and perpetrated the crucifixion.

But why should I speak of this as if it were merely historical, distant and remote? For still so often He comes to His own and His own receive Him not. It is all of us together whose sins, worked out into social magnitudes, 'crucify Christ afresh and put Him to an open shame'. It is not God's will that I should do that—it is the devil's will. Yet, God pity me, I do it, and go on doing it.

Is there then no hope? There is! For that is only one side of the action. The other side is what God made and still makes of the passion of His Son. For out of that terrible experience Jesus came back, from the other side of the grave, and met the men whose betrayal and desertion had sold Him to that fate; and the word of this Joseph of the new covenant was this: 'Be not grieved nor angry with yourselves that you sold Me hither, for God sent Me before you, to save life.'

What a wonderful forgiveness! For us whose weak self-love and guilty pride have betrayed Him again and again, for us who have acted Peter and Iscariot and Pilate and Caiaphas and all the host of them, what a world-transforming forgiveness! Surely if God is to be found anywhere in the world, it is at the cross of Jesus. Call that cross the terrible result of a massive coalition of evil, call it the logical outcome of the way I live and you live and all the world lives—and that is true. But call it the mightiest of all the mighty acts of God, and the deeper truth stands revealed. This is God in action to save life, to save you and me and all mankind. Joseph, by humanly co-operating with an unseen purpose, became the saviour of his nation. Christ, by divinely identifying Himself with the eternal will, became the Redeemer of the world.

I began by saying that the most important thing about any man is his interpretation of life. Well, which is it? For there is obviously a real choice here. Here is the practical arena of decision in which, as Christians, we find ourselves.

Jesus won His victory—how? Because He saw, running right through creation and life and history one transcendent force, the will of God His Father; and because to the sweep and surge of that will He gave Himself utterly, concurring in it with every atom of His being. This surely was the secret of those hours of prayer and communion on the mountain top, when all the world was quiet; and this the outcome, when He descended to the crowded ways of men again—a will most perfectly attuned to the eternal purpose of His Father God.

This is the challenge. Let me put it as compellingly as I can. Take the first words of our Christian creed: 'I believe in God the Father Almighty, Maker of heaven and earth.' What does that mean? It means that over everything, penetrating, supporting, overruling everything, there is one tremendous fact—the will of God. Why is there a creation, a world, a cosmos, here at all? Because the Father Almighty, Maker of heaven and earth, resolved and willed it. What is it that holds the structured universe together, and which if it were withdrawn would lead to immediate and total disintegration? The pressure of the will of God. Running right through life, through time and space, nature and personality, history and experience, there is this one living incomparable energy, this supercharged cosmic current, the will of God.

And here is the challenge now. For this force, this energy, this living will that runs through all creation, runs through your life and experience too. Those good desires and aspirations that visit us from time to time—these are not just something thought up out of your own heads: they are the will of God touching us. Your love for the partner of your life—the will of God. Your service of the needy, your giving of yourself in outgoing helpfulness—the will of God. Your kneeling down to pray, your allowing the face of Christ to shine out at you from your prayers, your self-identification in prayer with Jesus, the desire of all nations and the hope of the ends of the earth, so that through you something of the work of the incarnation, some minute infinitesimal part of that work, still in you goes forward—that is the will of God.

I wonder if you feel, as I do, that it is an almost frightening thought. When I think of the vast will of God Almighty, which created and sustains and penetrates the inconceivable immensities of the universe, sun and moon and stars and all the galaxies of space, to say nothing of this earth, the will that has held creation in being from the first day until now; when I think of that supernatural force intersecting my life, at the very ground of my being, every day I live—I find it an awesome thought.

Yes, but glorious too, for Christ's revelation means that this will is ultimately love, and nothing but love. Here truth and love absolutely coincide. It means that in proportion as I yield to that will, and align myself to the rhythm of that mighty force sweeping through creation, I can be carried along by the same cosmic power that turned Christ's death and passion into resurrection and victory. It means that now if I take into my heart the Lord Jesus, committing my soul to One who is Himself the will of God incarnate, there are no difficulties that cannot be transformed, no trials that cannot yield their meaning, no joys that will not be a hundredfold enhanced, no sins that cannot be obliterated for ever, and in the end no shadow of death that cannot lead on beyond death to the sunburst of everlasting life. One day, through the grace of the new Joseph, the dear Lord Christ, I shall be able to say, looking back on all that life and death have done—'So now it was not you that brought me hither, but God!'

If this is not the gospel, there is no gospel at all. If this is not good news for you, for me, for all the sons of men, there is no news worth anything anywhere. This, nothing less, is the news we are met here to celebrate in worship. And our response?

> O make us worthy, gracious Lord,
> Of all Thy love to be;
> To Thy blest will our wills incline,
> That unto death we may be Thine,
> And ever live in Thee.

IX

A THREEFOLD ASSURANCE

'Blessed be the God and Father of our Lord Jesus Christ, who has blessed us in Christ with every spiritual blessing in the heavenly places, even as He chose us in Him before the foundation of the world, that we should be holy and blameless before Him. He destined us in love to be His sons through Jesus Christ, according to the purpose of His will, to the praise of His glorious grace which He freely bestowed on us in the Beloved. In Him we have redemption through His blood, the forgiveness of our trespasses, according to the riches of His grace which He lavished upon us. For He has made known to us in all wisdom and insight the mystery of His will, according to His purpose which He set forth in Christ as a plan for the fullness of time, to unite all things in Him, things in heaven and things on earth. In Him, according to the purpose of Him who accomplishes all things according to the counsel of His will, we who first hoped in Christ have been destined and appointed to live for the praise of His glory'—Ephesians 1:3-12 (R.S.V.).

If ever there was a time when it was essential that Christian people should be clear about their own faith, that time is today. Some of us who profess and call ourselves Christians have been too vague in our beliefs, too lacking in precision in the logic of our witness. Unless the Church is definite about the faith it holds—not indeed in the sense of 'knowing all the answers', but in being possessed by certain basic convictions—the world is likely to accord it precisely that measure of attention which such vagueness and uncertainty deserve, which is none whatever.

The Church has often in the past been criticised for arrogantly giving the impression that it knows all the answers. But certainly that is not the danger today, if ever it was. The danger today is the very opposite. The danger is that we Christians should be so self-consciously eager to plead 'Not Guilty' to dogmatism in theology and authoritarianism in ethics, so anxious to make concessions to a pluralist society's diversity of views, that we deliberately soft-pedal some of the gospel's characteristic notes. There is a real danger of the Church being stampeded into capitulation to its secular environment, and specially to secularism's notorious antipathy to any idea of an invasion of the historical order and the human scene by a living and transcendent Creator Spirit. It is thus that we have tended to be too vague and nebulous in our beliefs.

So let us suppose this. Suppose that a sincere agnostic searching for the light were to ask, 'What is this faith you profess? What is the new life you claim? Exactly what difference does it make?' Could we set down our answer quite specifically on half a sheet of notepaper? Or should we have to adopt evasive action, with perhaps some muddled plea about preferring not to be dogmatic?

How different with the men of the New Testament! No vague hesitation there. 'I was blind: He gave me sight.' 'I was lost: He sought and found me.' 'I was beaten and bewildered and at the end of my tether: He gave me the spirit of victory.' 'I was earthbound and corrupt: He gave me the dimension of eternity.' This is the testimony.

Let us turn to St. Paul, whose voice amongst all these others rings out like a trumpet-note. The magnificent prologue to Ephesians runs on for a dozen verses without a break, a lyrical doxology to the praise of Him 'who has blessed us in Christ with every spiritual blessing'. 'You ask me what I owe,' says Paul in effect. 'I answer there is nothing I do not owe. God gave me everything—every manner of blessing—when He gave me Christ.' And then from all this profusion of blessing the apostle singles out three things, three specific and stupendous facts. These are for him the very core and centre of the faith, the certainties on which his life was built.

First, *the call of God*: the divine election. 'He chose us in Christ before the foundation of the world.'

God has chosen us. This is the Christian valuation, the startling, staggering estimate of those lives that often seem drab and ordinary and disappointing and depressing. God has elected us in Christ.

It is tragically unfortunate that this great cardinal truth of the divine calling and election, which runs right through the New

Testament from start to finish, has been persistently misunder-stood and misinterpreted, sometimes even with grim, sub-Christian ideas imported into and superimposed upon it by harsh and truculent theologies. Let us be clear once for all that in everything it says about divine election the New Testament has one paramount concern, and one only: namely, to proclaim beyond the shadow of a doubt that salvation—yours, mine, any-one's, the whole world's—is always and everywhere the sovereign act of the living God. Not by chance nor accident does faith spring up within a human soul. It is not my choice that lands me in the Kingdom of God. There is nothing in us that even remotely explains our place in Christ's discipleship. We have not earned it. We have not qualified for it. We have not worked up to it. You know that this I am saying is true. You know in your own heart it is true. There has been a higher will at work. 'You have not chosen Me: I have chosen you.' That is it. To God be the glory!

This is what the New Testament is driving at when it speaks of election. This is what Paul means here. 'He chose us as His own in Christ before the foundation of the world.' Do you see how practical this is? What a marvellous confidence it ought to give us to know that our place in the Christian fellowship today has behind it, not any chance collocation of human circumstances, but God's eternal will! When I am feeling disappointed and ashamed and ready to drop out of the fight, wondering whether my place in the Christian discipleship is not perhaps a huge pre-posterous mistake, what a relief to be set free from that dangerous subjectivity into a cleansing, healing recollection of the sovereign grace of God! What an immense and powerful reinforcement to hear the word from heaven: 'I have chosen you. I have made an everlasting covenant with you, and will stand by it to the end!'

Observe, too, what this signifies on the wider scale of the world. It is a terrible world to look out on today if you see only the human factors, only men and nations desperately trying to work out a precarious salvation. What a lost and crazy world it is, with its strange mingling of technological affluence and achieve-ment on the one hand and spiritual impoverishment and famine on the other, and with its demonic playing with nuclear fire and the devilry of biological warfare! Certainly there would seem to be ample grounds for fatalism, cynicism and despair.

But a Christian, looking out on the darkened scene, retains unshadowed confidence, because he knows there is another factor in the field and a greater will constantly and unwearyingly at work: the immense pressure of a transcendent penetrating energy that fills the universe and every detail of creation. 'God so loved,' said Jesus—not just one favoured segment of the human race, not Israel or the Church, not the well-meaning or the spiritually-minded—'God so loved the world.' Time enough to despair of history when the Creator God who brought history into being has abdicated the throne. Time enough to start losing heart when Christ the Word incarnate confesses that His passion was a blunder and the truth He taught a lie. Till then, son of man, stand upon your feet, believing in the divine initiative and recognising the unslumbering pressure in every instant of a supreme and sovereign grace. For God has chosen this world to be at last the Kingdom of His Son.

This, then, is the first great thing Paul sets down as the core of his faith and the certainty on which his life was built: the call of God. Let us pass on to what follows.

He tells us, in the second place, that our holy faith includes this: *the charter of sonship*. His own term here is adoption. 'He destined us in love to be His sons through Jesus Christ.' Through Christ, you are adopted into the family. By union with Christ, you become a son of God.

In a sense, of course, it is true that all men are God's children, simply by virtue of being alive in God's world. But there are different kinds of life, different levels and dimensions of existence. There is the level of inorganic matter; then the level of organic life, in plants and flowers; above that again, the level of sentient life, in animals. Finally, above that, there is our life on earth as human beings, with intelligence, emotion and will, the order of existence into which we are born, our nature. But the whole force of Christianity is concentrated on this—that there is a higher level of life than nature: there is super-nature, a fourth-dimensional quality of life, the very life that is in God Himself; and that if we are born of God—His sons and daughters—this life can be ours.

This is the revolutionary thing about Christianity. Some there are who still imagine that what Christianity is primarily concerned with is ethical guide-lines, moral values and decent behaviour. What a dull business churchgoing would be, if that were all you could hear about! It is far more explosive and dynamic than that. It is the offer to men—to you and me—not just of an improved quality of existence, but actually of the very life of God Himself. No wonder the New Testament throbs with excitement from end to end! No wonder these men of the Testament are overwhelmingly eager to share the tremendous news. For if God's supernatural life—this new dimension, this extra capacity—comes to be in men, then obviously anything becomes possible. There could be victory over any fierce temptation. There could be the potentiality of the resolving even of the most frightful and colossal international dilemmas.

If! But how? Have we to climb up to this higher life by our own poor stumbling efforts? That is utterly and for ever impossible. In the nature of the case, it cannot happen. If we are to share this life, it must come down to us. And that, says Christianity, is precisely the way God has taken.

When God became man, the unbridgeable gulf was bridged. Right in the heart of the human race, the supernatural life has appeared. What constitutes the gospel is the self-communication of God. It is not just that Christ shows me what I ought to be: it is that, in proportion as I lay myself open to Him, He shares His life, which is God's life, with me, imparting it to me as the vine injects its life into the branch. Thus—as the Bible puts it— we can be transformed into His likeness, and grow up into Him. Thus the Son of God makes us sons of God indeed.

This is one indispensable significance of churchgoing—that, in worship, Christ our great High Priest draws us into direct communion with God, and that thus our exhausted energies and wayward souls are replenished from the source of all true life. This is the charter of sonship. This, nothing less, is what is offered in the gospel.

Come, almighty to deliver;
Let us all Thy life receive.

We have now seen two great things which Paul in these shin-ing sentences has set down as the core of the faith and the cer-tainty on which his life was built. We pass finally to the third: *the conquest of evil.* 3

For inevitably the objection will be raised: 'All very well to talk of the call of God and the charter of sonship, election and adoption. That might be conceivable if the record were clean. It might be credible if man and his history had never known corrup-tion. But are you facing the facts? For manifestly something has gone radically wrong: there is a tragic disharmony at the centre, a cosmic dislocation. The world is such that there can be beastly horrors in it like poison gas, racialism, violence, malnutrition and starvation and the mounting menace of pollution. The human heart is such that its best aspirations are shadowed by the blight and rot of evil. Can there be any exit from this vicious circle, any solution of the terrible dilemma?'

It is a real challenge. And it was to meet this demand that Paul, having presented two cardinal grounds of Christian assur-ance—the call of God, the charter of sonship—proceeds now to set down the third: 'In Him we have redemption through His blood, the forgiveness of sins.' In Christ there is the assurance of the conquest of evil.

If we understood this as the men of the New Testament did, their amazed adoring wonder would be ours. It is indeed a stupendous assertion—that upon the tangled and pathetic human scene of frustration, corruption, perdition and death, God Himself has arrived, and taken action to put us right and set us free. And the marvel grows as you watch how the mighty act of liberation was accomplished. Not by ignoring evil, not by making light of its diabolically self-propagating influence: that would be demoralising sentimentalism, not holy love. That was not Jesus' attitude. But by taking the evil upon Himself and absorb-ing it, by allowing it to work itself out to its devastating uttermost in His own body and soul, by experiencing the perdition of man as if it were His own—by this terrible cost He drew the sting of evil, broke its tyranny and destroyed its despotism. 'In Him,' declares Paul, 'we have redemption through His blood, the for-giveness of sins, according to the riches of His grace.'

Yes, if we choose to take it. Yes, if we are united to Christ by \

Concl

an act of personal and self-identifying commitment. Without that, God's mighty works in the gospel have for us been done in vain, a far-off uncertain rumour, nothing more. The new life achieved by the cross and the resurrection remains beyond our possession. Union with Jesus Christ—this is the crux of everything, the union of which Paul could say, 'Christ liveth in me.' Just as He took on Himself my weakness, my inadequacy, my defeat, so now through the Spirit I take His power, His victory, His peace.

Have you ever noticed how often one little phrase occurs in the addresses at the beginning of Paul's letters? It is immensely significant. 'In Corinth, in Christ.' 'In Colosse, in Christ.' 'In Philippi, in Christ.' This is the apostle reminding those Christians and reminding us of our true life-situation: 'in Christ', in faith-union with the living Lord. It runs right through the passage we have been studying. Would it not be well, when so much is being said and written nowadays about 'situation ethics', to remember that this, nothing less, is the total situation of the Church, the true locus of the Christian: in the secular world indeed, but also and quite definitely in Christ?

Paul knew what he was talking about—Paul who could say both 'I am a Roman citizen' and 'My citizenship is in heaven.' Some would deny the simultaneity of the twofold environment. They would say: 'Either you can be in Ephesus but not in Christ—which is secularism; or you can be in Christ but not in Ephesus—which is monasticism.' Paul would say it is precisely because you are in Ephesus that you need to be in Christ; and that it is precisely by being in Christ that Ephesus comes to have new meaning.

The real objection to much of the argument for situation ethics is not that it goes too far, but that it does not go far enough. You must take the total situation, not just a fraction of it; and certainly for the Church, and for each individual Christian incorporated by baptism, the major part of the situation is that contained in the words 'in Christ'. At any given moment in the life of the Church, in every single instant in the life of the believer, this is the situation—surrounded by, immersed in, the same energy of life and light and love which penetrates and sustains the whole vast structure of creation, and in which the unthinkable immensities of the universe cohere. This is the situation: 'your life,' as Paul expresses it, 'hidden with Christ in God': each tiny cell of the Body of Christ filled with the pulse and power of the Spirit, each microcosmic existence penetrated by the love that moves the sun and all the stars.

This is the secret of the life of the redeemed, life eternal here and now in the midst of time. This is the inbreaking into history of the kingdom of heaven. This is the darkness routed and the night gone, and the glory of the Lord risen upon us.

Concl:
The situation of the Christian is that he is in Christ — "each tiny cell"

X

THE DIVINE IN THE HUMAN

'I have seen thy face, as though I had seen the face of God'—
Genesis 33:10.

What a dramatic confrontation this is! Jacob's words to Esau
are very quiet, restrained, utterly simple, yet throbbing with the
deepest feeling. The two brothers had met after long estrange-
ment. Years before, Jacob, in the matter of the birthright, had
taken a dastardly advantage of his brother, had wronged him
frightfully. Jacob then had lived up to his name—the twister,
the deceiver. He saw that now. His conscience during the inter-
vening years had been smiting him, telling him that on that
earlier occasion he had acted shabbily and shamefully. Under-
standably, then, Jacob had not been looking forward to this meeting. It was likely to be most uncomfortable. There was almost
bound to be a painful scene. He wished he did not have to go
through with it. He would not have gone through with it if it
had not been for a strange inner compulsion. But when the
dreaded hour actually arrived, Jacob could hardly believe his
eyes and ears. Could it be true? Esau magnanimously refused
to cherish any grudge, and offered without question a right hand
of fellowship. No wonder Jacob, receiving that free and un-
deserved forgiveness, was moved to the depths of his being. He
felt that here he was in the presence of something truly divine.
'I have seen thy face, as though I had seen the face of God.'

Now this is no old Bible story merely. It is an experience which,
in varying forms, happens to most of us on our journey through
this world. For very often it is at the point of our personal
relationships that the living God impinges on us. It is through
our human contacts that we become aware of the touch of the
divine. The Word is made flesh, the eternal looks out at us
through human eyes, the divine reassuring love speaks to us in

human tones; and with Jacob we can say—'I have seen thy face, as though I had seen the face of God.'

There is indeed a revelation of another kind, the revelation that comes through the world of nature. It would be strange if we could say that God has never spoken to us there. Listen in this connection to just one voice among many, the voice of that gay and gallant spirit Edward Wilson, who died with Captain Scott in the Antarctic. 'A happy life,' he wrote in one of his letters, 'is not built up of tours abroad and pleasant holidays, but of little clumps of violets noticed by the roadside, hidden away almost, so that only those can see them who have God's peace and love in their hearts; in one long continuous chain of little joys; little whispers from the spiritual world, little gleams of sunshine on our daily work. So long as I have stuck to nature and the New Testament, I have only got happier every day.' And one does not need to be a Wilson or a Wordsworth to share that insight, and to see past the world of created nature to the Creator Spirit whose power and wisdom it reflects.

Is it not then to be expected that if God can draw so near through inanimate nature He should draw even nearer through living persons? For personality is the highest category that we know. It is a great thing when a man can look at the world, the inanimate world around, and say 'I have seen God there': but it is a greater thing when a husband, for instance, can look into the face of his wife and say, 'My beloved, I have seen God in you.' We have listened to Edward Wilson of the Antarctic testifying how God came to him through nature. But here is something else from the same pen, on the last long journey from which he never returned. It is from a letter to his wife. 'I get an hour to myself, as a rule, before breakfast, when I am quite alone; and then I sometimes pray, sometimes read your letters and write to you; and I feel it is all communion with God.' Is that not a noble testimony to what human fellowship can do to reveal and embody the divine? 'It is all communion with God.' And it does not stand alone. Is there one of us who has never felt, through the medium of personal relationships, the authentic touch of God upon his soul? 'The peace of God,' said Tennyson of his wife, 'came into my heart before the altar on the day I wedded her.'

God is so much nearer than we sometimes think. There are indeed multitudes of people today wondering whether there is any Creator Spirit anywhere, any beneficent Providence to control the fierce anarchic element in life and to give meaning to the jumble of their own experience, crying inarticulately like Job long ago—'O that I knew where I might find Him!' What do they expect? Is it some spectacular sign in the heavens, some miraculous unearthly voice ringing through the dark? That is not God's way of self-disclosure. But there is an unwritten saying of Jesus which the memory of some unknown Christian preserved from oblivion: 'Jesus said, "Thou hast seen thy brother; thou hast seen thy Lord." ' And that means that you do not need (as the psalmist put it) to ascend into the heavens or take the wings of the morning to the uttermost parts of the seas, or anything dramatic like that at all, to come upon God; for He is there all the time in your most intimate personal relationships. 'Thou hast seen thy brother: then thou hast seen thy Lord.' The personal relation is the point of the divine impact.

But so often we persist in frustrating the grace of heaven by looking for God in the wrong place. Think of it like this. Suppose you are in trouble, and you pray God to come and help you. 'Lord, here am I. Here is this deep darkness that has come upon me. Help me through the difficult place—help me for Thy tender mercies' sake.' What do you expect to happen? Well, Paul was once in that precise situation. Paul was in the thick of trouble, dreadful trouble, and he prayed God to come and comfort him. 'Lord, here am I, Your servant Paul, tossed about with many a conflict, many a doubt, fightings and fears, within, without.' What happened to that prayer? The door opened and in walked—not an angel, not the risen living Christ—but a man called Titus, quite an ordinary man, not even a particularly distinguished man, just a friend, with a rallying word and an understanding heart. But somehow he had not been there ten minutes before Paul knew his prayer was answered and his problem solved; and writing later to the Corinthian Church he said, 'God, who comforteth those who are cast down, comforted me by the coming of Titus.' God—not Titus—did it. It was the Lord Himself who had come that night to the apostle's door—'Behold, I stand at the door and knock'—God through the personal relationship.

And it is not only when one prays for comfort that this kind of thing can happen. Perhaps you pray for guidance in a difficult situation, and God sends a friend to talk it out with you: and that is God's answer. Perhaps you pray for God's forgiveness, and someone when you are feeling wretched treats you as a brother: and that is God's answer. Perhaps you pray for a second chance when you have been defeated, and someone goes on believing in you: and that is God's answer.

Mark you, I am not denying that God can strike into our experience directly, without any intermediary—like the blinding flash of light that came to Saul of Tarsus at Damascus. That can and does happen—thank God it does.

But for the moment I am thinking about God's other way; and I am begging you not to miss the voice of heaven, not to think the revelation any less valid or authentic, when it comes, as so often it does come, through human relationships. 'You're Christ to me,' cried the dying soldier in the Crimea to Florence Nightingale as she went round the ward at night carrying her lamp, 'you're Christ to me'—then he fell back and died. And Augustine had the same experience about Monica. It was said about a veteran Scots missionary returned from Livingstonia that there was something about Dr. Donald Fraser's smile which on a grey day would light up a rainswept Glasgow or Edinburgh street— and those of us who knew Donald Fraser would homologate that from the heart. In every congregation there are people who would testify that they have found in human love and sympathy and understanding the authentic touch of the divine, and the assurance that 'underneath are the everlasting arms'. 'I have seen thy face, as though I had seen the face of God.'

Let me make this more particular by asking you to think of just two divine attributes, two apparently contrasted elements in the being of God.

Think, on the one hand, of the divine holiness. You may say —and rightly—that that is an abstract conception, difficult to apprehend. But you have looked into the face of a little child, and felt the stabbing challenge of that innocence and purity, as though God Himself were looking out at you. Is there not in the eyes of a child something to reinforce our best aspirations, to rebuke and reproach our compromising ways, something to sanctify the soul within us? That is the divine holiness incarnate, the Word made flesh: so that you can take a little child into your arms and say, meaning every word of it, 'I have seen thy face, as though I had seen the face of God.'

Did not Robert Browning, in his dramatic poem 'Pippa Passes', give us a magnificent commentary on this? The spiritual insight of that poem is marvellous. It is the story of how a child, singing her happy way down the street, brought first one life and then another (though she herself knew nothing about it) face to face with God, the Holy One. In one street there was a house where a soul was being terribly tempted, on the very edge and precipice of sin; and past that house of Ottima and Sebald went Pippa, singing her song—

> The year's at the spring,
> And day's at the morn;
> Morning's at seven;
> The hillside's dew-pearled;
> The lark's on the wing;
> The snail's on the thorn;
> God's in His heaven—
> All's right with the world!

And that unconscious song struck straight into Sebald's soul, and brought a swift revulsion from his sin. 'God's in His heaven,' he cried out of the depths of his dawning remorse, 'Do you hear that? God's in His heaven!'

> That little peasant's voice
> Has righted all again. Though I be lost,
> I know which is the better, never fear,
> Of vice or virtue. God's in His heaven!

So Pippa went upon her way; and before that day was done, through the voice of a little child, one here and another there had encountered, down the secret by-ways of apostasy and defeat, the reproachful and redeeming face of the Lord of all good life.

And it is not only a child who can do that. All the pure things of this world, all the men and women who are clean-souled and loyal, have that power. In them the Word is being made flesh. The divine holiness stands at our door and knocks with human hands: and when we open—'I have seen thy face, as though I had seen the face of God.'

Think now of the other attribute, the apparently contrasted element in the being and nature of God: the divine mercy and compassion. That again may sound abstract and intangible and remote. But have you never been forgiven by someone, and felt that in that very act you were being reconciled to God? It was this, as we have seen, that first brought the cry of our text to Jacob's lips. It was the amazingly magnanimous forgiveness embodied in his brother Esau which mirrored and made credible for him the forgiveness of God.

Let me set alongside this another, even more dramatic instance, from the New Testament. Do you remember that moment in the Book of Acts when a good man, a Christian called Ananias, found Saul of Tarsus just after his conversion lying blind and stunned and helpless in a house in Damascus? Saul, as Ananias well knew, was the dreadful, notorious character who had been cursing the name of Jesus, harrying the Church, staining his hands in Christian blood. Was it not mad to think that such a one could be brought into the Christian fellowship? Surely there must be a preposterous mistake somewhere, or even some dark devilish device. But this good man Ananias accepted the unlikely commission. He sought Saul out and found him, and his first words were 'Brother Saul'. No wonder we read immediately afterwards, 'There fell from Saul's eyes as it had been scales.' Brother Saul! It was that amazing, humbling forgiveness for all the cruelty and violence of the past, that right hand of fellowship into the community he had been persecuting to the death, which interpreted and made credible for Paul the forgiveness of God.

And on more ordinary levels of life this is going on all the time. The Word is made flesh, the remote abstraction becomes concrete and alive in human form, the mercy of heaven encompasses you with human hands: and you look into the eyes of someone, shining for you with steadfast lovingkindness and generous understanding. 'I have seen thy face, as though I had seen the face of God.'

But now, look where our thoughts have led us. Have they not been carrying us to the very threshold of the mystery of the Incarnation? For everything we have been thinking of is summed up in Christ. He is the friend, His is the friendship, that bring God to us supremely.

See how it happened for His own disciples. At first their thoughts of Him were dim and groping; but as time went on, and as they lived longer in His company, strange things began to happen. I imagine Peter and John talking together one night when the day's journeying was over. 'Do you know, John,' said Peter, 'when I say my prayers to God at nights, somehow it is the Master's face that keeps rising before my mind.' And John would reply, 'Yes, Peter, I have found the very same. And do you remember how we saw Him the other day with the little children clambering to His arms? It suddenly reminded me of what Isaiah says about the Lord God—God carrying the lambs in His bosom!' 'Yes, John, and all those other days we have seen Him laying His hands on lepers' sores, speaking kinder words to sinful folk than human ears have ever hoped to hear, quelling raging evil spirits and dangerous demons, making the least, the loneliest and the lost feel there is one heart that loves them still, bearing their griefs and carrying their sorrows: I tell you that always the thought that keeps growing stronger in my mind is this—there is something divine, transcendent, supernatural in this Friend of ours. He has brought God Himself before our eyes.' So I imagine the two disciples talking together. And so the story ran on to the end. They all saw their Master dying at the last with forgiveness on His lips, saw Him royal and undiminished even in death, saw Him coming back to them from the last darkness, a living risen presence at their sides, on the Emmaus road, in the upper room, and beside their homely highland loch in Galilee. And this was what they went forth into all the world to proclaim: 'We have seen His face, and lo, it is the face of God. We preach Christ Jesus, God made visible.'

Will you think just once again of those two contrasted

attributes—the divine holiness, the divine mercy? Is it not in Jesus that they both lay hold of us?

The divine inflexible holiness. There was a gifted young artist who in wartime was billeted as a soldier in a hut in France with a score of other men. Some of them had placarded on the walls of their hut pictures of a coarse and offensive kind. The young artist was a Christian, and he hated it. He was in a dilemma. He knew that mere protesting would achieve nothing. But one night, when the hut was quiet and his companions asleep, he got out a candle and a pencil and a bit of paper about the size of a post-card, and began to draw the head of Jesus Christ. He had some-times tried to paint a picture of Christ before, and always he knew he had failed. But now he tried again. When it was finished, he put it on the wall above his own bed. He wondered what the others would say in the morning when they saw it. Morning came, and they saw it. Nothing was said at all. But within a week every other picture had somehow vanished from the walls, and only that face of Christ remained. The other things just could not live beside it. It is thus that in Jesus the divine holiness con-fronts us. There is nothing so cleansing and strengthening, so sure a defence in the day of danger, as one steady look at the face of Jesus. There are some things that just cannot happen when He is there. Jesus, Master, I have seen Thy face, and I know I have seen the holiness of God.

And if it is thus that the divine holiness encounters us, is the same not also true of the divine mercy? We sometimes find it difficult to believe God can forgive us, so deeply are we im-plicated in the sinfulness of humanity, so mixed with earth our most celestial motives. How can forgiving love get through? If indeed it could have been that Jesus were here today, if this could have been not a church in Edinburgh but the beach at Capernaum and we could have heard Him saying, as He said of old, 'I love you and am your Friend for ever—rise up and follow Me'; if we could have climbed Calvary and heard Him cry 'Father, forgive them, for they know not what they do'—do you not think that would have changed our thoughts of God? Well, He *is* here, and He *is* saying it; and can you doubt the heart of God when you are looking at the face of Jesus?

There was a scoffing sceptic who entered a church in Paris

during the singing of part of the Mass: 'Agnus Dei, qui tollis peccata mundi'—Lamb of God, who takest away the sins of the world. As he listened, something got beneath his scepticism and quenched his scoffing: 'O God,' he exclaimed, 'what a dream! Taking away the sins of the world indeed—what a dream! And yet—and yet—if only He could!' I tell you now—He can. He has done precisely that. I look at my sins, and it is incredible God should ever forgive them. But I look at Jesus, and immediately I know that the incredible has happened. I have seen Thy face, O Christ, as though I had seen the face of God. 'As though'? No, not that any longer. Far better than that! There is no 'as if' or 'as though' about it. I *have* seen the face of God the Father. And as is His majesty, so is His mercy. O Word made flesh, how can I ever praise Thee enough for this? Thanks be to God for His unspeakable gift!

XI

ON MAKING FAITH EXPLICIT

'All I know is this: once I was blind, now I can see'—John 9:25 (N.E.B.).

It was a saying of John Ruskin's that you 'ought to imagine yourself present, as in the body, at each recorded act in the life of Redeemer'. Take any scene in the Gospels: you are to imagine yourself there when it happened, actually looking on as a spectator on the spot, watching, listening, seeing the whole drama. That is the advice, and as far as it goes it is helpful.

As far as it goes. For what it fails to tell us is this: the detached spectator position, when we try to occupy it, is ruled out by the Gospels themselves. The spectator is suddenly made to realise that he is a participant in the scene. He is not simply there looking on: he is himself involved in the action. He is identified now with this character on the stage, now with that other; in fact, in some mysterious way he is identified with all of them. There is something of himself in each of them.

Here, for example, is this story presented to us by St. John. The blind man groping for the light—who is he? Myself. Those disciples, with their stupid and misguided questioning? Myself. Those finical Pharisees, with their built-in traditionalism? Myself.

This is the extraordinary thing the Gospels are always doing: you want a place in the stalls—a spectator, a bystander, a looker-on —and the Gospels say, 'No! You come right up here, for this is your life: your place is here in the drama.'

So I do not need to argue for the relevance of this story today. This man at the Judean roadside is just ourselves. We are all blind, until God in Christ has made us see. _Intro_

Without that, we cannot see ourselves as we really are, cannot see our brother-man as he truly is, cannot see the meaning and wonder and purpose of life, 'earth crammed with heaven and every common bush afire with God'.

Until then, we are blind: and the proofs of it are the illusions we human creatures cherish, the prejudices we mistake for truth, the dull familiarity of things that gets us down in miserable depression. Blind—because every mistake we make does something more to atrophy the faculty of vision, and every moral compromise progressively desensitises the soul. And when men or nations think to build a new order and a better world, with God nowhere in their thoughts, they are simply—as Jesus Himself put it—'the blind leading the blind, and both will fall into the ditch'. This blind man at the roadside is just ourselves, until God in Christ has laid His hand upon us.

Now watch Jesus' disciples. We are here too. To them, this pathetic object at the roadside was primarily a theological problem. 'Who did sin, this man or his parents, that he was born blind?' That is to say, those disciples found focused here the problem of evil and the mystery of suffering, the perennial 'Why?' Why should life have this dark, ominous streak across it? If God at creation 'saw everything that He had made, and behold, it was very good', why has the process gone so terribly astray that there can be refugees and atom bombs and slums and men born blind?

Well, there was an answer that the current Jewish theology would certainly have given. The Rabbis had their rigid theory about such cases: every misfortune a direct punishment for individual or corporate wrongdoing—either the wrongdoing of others, or some mysterious pre-natal wrongdoing of the individual himself. That was the formula.

But look! Jesus will not accept it. Once for all He sets aside the orthodox notion of an equivalence between suffering and sin —that theory which still lingers and cruelly haunts so many in the time of trouble, making them feel miserably 'Am I the chief of sinners that this suffering has come to me?' Jesus sets it aside peremptorily as being too crude and superficial to fit the facts. He makes it obsolete. 'Neither did this man sin, nor his parents.'

Having said that—notice this, for it is immensely significant —He does not pursue further the question as to the origins of the tragic element in life. He leaves it alone. Indeed, His next

words practically say to the disciples—that is, to you and me—
'You are asking the wrong question altogether. Neither did this
man sin nor his parents: but that the works of God should be
made manifest in him, I must now do the work of Him who sent
Me.'

Do you catch His meaning? He is turning to His followers and
saying—'You are too abstract in your theology. You are asking,
Where does responsibility for this situation lie? Can we put our
finger on it and say—That is where it has come from?' Now of
course Jesus does not rule out the importance of that effort to
track down evil and trace it to its roots in order to deal with it
and if possible to eliminate it. But He says there is something
even more immediate. 'What you ought to be asking,' He says,
'is not, How did this situation arise? It is, Seeing this situation
is here, how can we let God in upon it now, so that God's will
takes control? For in every situation, however dark, that is always
possible. The works of God can be manifested right here!'

It is vitally important to be clear about this. Make it quite
personal. Suppose some sudden trouble comes on you, and you
then start asking 'Why has this come? Why have I to suffer in
this way?'—well, you may be able to answer, or you may not.
Even Jesus will not always answer that. But what He wants you
to see is that, whether or not you can explain why the harsh
discipline has fallen to your lot, it is always possible, now that
it has presented itself, to do something about it, namely, to let
God in upon it, and so to use it positively and creatively. In other
words, there are no irreparable disasters when faith takes charge,
no conceivable situation in which there does not exist some opportunity of glorifying God. And those who have learnt this are
conquerors in the fight.

Come back to the story. The blind eyes are anointed, the man
is sent to wash in the healing waters, and suddenly—the incredible
happens. Do try to imagine it—the swift shattering of the darkness of a lifetime, the opening of the sightless eyes—for this is
the characteristic work of Jesus still, for you and me and all the
world. For the first time in his life, this man sees—what? Four
things.

He sees the world around him—that first—the wonder and

beauty of God's creation. He sees the faces of his fellow men—
that next. He sees himself, his hands, his feet, his face (if there was
a mirror handy), showing him what kind of a man he was. And
finally (a little later in the story) he sees Jesus, to whom he owes
it all.

Are these not precisely the four facts to which Christ opens our
eyes today? He opens our eyes to the world, so that we can see
the glory of God in His creation: sun and sky, trees and flowers,
rivers and mountains, they are all my Father's making. He opens
our eyes to our fellow men—so that we do not think of them any
more as faces in the street or cogs in a machine or factors in a
race problem: every one is now a child of God, a brother for
whom Christ died. He opens our eyes to ourselves—a humbling,
disillusioning process, and yet the way to penitence and pardon
and peace. And this above all: He opens our eyes to Himself,
so that He is no longer Someone we read about in a book or
hear of in church or argue about in a discussion group, but the
living centre of our lives, the one true light to irradiate and
interpret everything else. A new vision of creation, of our brother-
man, of ourselves, of Christ—all that, when the Lord who is
the Light of the world has touched us and made us see.

What next? This—you have it in verses 8 to 12—the man
is interrogated by his neighbours. Mark that well: for if Christ's
Spirit has once entered your life, people are bound to notice it.
They ought to notice it. So it was here. The neighbours ask
questions. 'How were your eyes opened?' He answered, 'A man
called Jesus did it.' Well, that was fairly vague, was it not? Not
Son of God, not Messiah, not even a great Rabbi: 'a man called
Jesus'. It could not have been much more rudimentary. So the
neighbours ask a second question: 'Where is He now?' He said,
'I know not.' In other words, this man was healed by a Christ
about whom he knew comparatively little. Now that I find both
encouraging and disconcerting.

Encouraging—why? Because it tells me that saving faith can
be a quite simple thing. You do not need any elaborate intricacies
of doctrine for a beginning. Jesus had said to this man, 'Go, wash
in Siloam,' and he was willing at least to try; but beyond that,
his whole apparatus of faith was inchoate and naïve. 'A man

48197

called Jesus.' 'Where is He now? I don't know.' And yet, on these terms, Christ gave him sight. Do you not see the tremendous hope there is in that—especially today when multitudes of people with only the vaguest theology are dimly aware of the moral issues posed by Jesus, when perhaps some here in this church now are wishing they could believe? Give Him the simplest faith, the first grammar of assent, and mighty works can happen still.

Yes, it is encouraging, this feature of the story; and yet, looked at from another angle, is it not also disconcerting? Here was a healed man who did not know who or where his Healer was. Here was a man incalculably in Christ's debt, yet not properly acknowledging it. Is that not all too familiar? So many of us in this country today are living on the Christian capital of past generations, with our code of ethics and our scale of values and our ways of thought coloured and conditioned at almost every point by the pervasive influence of Christ through nineteen centuries— yet not acknowledging, perhaps even repudiating, our debt. Are not some of us Church members far more vague and indifferent than we have any right to be about the source of life's supremest blessing? God make our faith articulate!

But now notice what it was that brought this man's faith to full articulation: it is very surprising and paradoxical. What had that effect was opposition, persecution. It was the attempt of the critics to discredit the miracle. It was this that made his faith explicit.

Look, then, at the emergent opposition. For we are in this too. Is it not strange that Christ cannot ever do a work of grace and blessing without someone being found to disparage it? That every forward movement of the faith accentuates the opposition?

Perhaps on second thoughts it is not quite so strange after all. For if this world is indeed the battle-ground of light and darkness, then every fresh advance of Christ exasperates the enemy, and every triumph of His Spirit is anathema. It is well to realise this, and be prepared. Always there will be voices to discount every miracle; always hands to pour cold water on every fire; always rationalising arguments to deflate every sense of the supernatural; always a counter-offensive to every triumph of the Lord. There was a Herod even at the cradle.

Look at it here. What explains the opposition of these people? Why did they bait and badger the poor soul? Ostensibly it was because Jesus had dared to heal him on the Sabbath. But of course that technical violation of the law was not the real reason: there was a considerable element of humbug about it. What really angered and infuriated them was the fact that here, going about the streets, would be yet another living proof of the power of Jesus. It was the thought—'Wherever this man goes, people will point at him and say, There is positive evidence that this new Healer comes from God!' That, to the critics, was the intolerable thing—as it still is today to the militant opponents of the faith. That instigated the opposition.

But now, here is the suggestive feature of the story: it was precisely the pressure of opposition that made this man an out-and-out believer. The cross-questioning he was subjected to had exactly the opposite effect to what was intended: it made a man of him, a real disciple.

Perhaps we all need a touch of opposition to make our religion vital. G. K. Chesterton declared it was reading the arguments of the sceptics that persuaded him of the truth of Christianity. I can imagine a young man who has always been vaguely on the Christian side, though never noticeably a Christian witness—and then one day something is said to bring Christ's name into contempt. Suddenly he feels, 'I can't stand this': and out comes his word of confession, his personal defence of the faith—the opposition making his dumb faith articulate. This is the challenge today. For it is not just apathy that the Christian faith is encountering now: in some quarters at least, even in this so-called Christian land, it is downright opposition and hostility. God make our faith explicit!

This man at any rate was not going to be browbeaten out of his conviction. His parents, you will observe, were really frightened of these disapproving and vituperative Pharisees. His parents, when asked pointedly, 'Is this your son? You allege he was born blind? How then does he see?'—were shivering in their shoes. They started stammering and stuttering and disclaiming any knowledge of what had happened—the flight to agnosticism —and ended up by saying, 'He is of age: ask him!' But the man himself was different. He refused to be intimidated or abashed. 'All I know is this: once I was blind, now I can see.'

That was as much as to say—You can argue till Doomsday that nothing has happened. You can use all the syllogisms of your logic to demonstrate that the alleged power of Jesus is myth and moonshine and delusion. You can prove to your own satisfaction that I am nothing but the pathetic victim of an unintelligent hallucination. Talk of intelligence? It is you who are the unintelligent ones! Do you not know the difference between light and darkness? All your fine arguments are wrecked on this: 'One thing I know, that whereas I was blind now I see!'

It is of course the unanswerable argument. If the Christian case were simply based on theory, it could doubtless by theory be demolished. If it were just a psychological phenomenon, the psychologists could tear it to shreds. But because it is based on actual events and history, on solid facts—lives redeemed, men made new, blindness turned to seeing—because of that, there is nothing that can shake it: it stands in its own right. I should like to set down this blind man beside some of our modern sceptics who deny the supernatural: he would soon make their scepticism look callow. This is the victory that overcomes all the sceptic voices of the world: 'One thing I know—once I was blind, now I can see.'

And now, the end of the story. I pass over all the vivid touches in between: how these persistent critics return to the attack; how the man, waxing bolder still, lets them feel the rapier of his irony—'Why are you questioning me like this about Jesus? Is it because you are proposing to become His disciples yourselves?' —a truly stinging gibe; how they angrily repudiate the taunt, even to the extent of casting aspersions on Jesus' character; how all the time his creed is growing more explicit—he began, you remember, with that studied vagueness, 'A man called Jesus' (v. 11), then a little later, 'A prophet' (v. 17), and now 'Someone from God' (v. 33)—so that he seems hovering on the verge of a full confession; how thereupon his cross-examiners, with a sudden burst of outraged pride—'Are you presuming to teach us?'— cast him out, that is, excommunicate him from the synagogue, ban him from communion. All that I pass over—but do read it again for yourselves, it is so fascinatingly vivid.

But just look at the conclusion of the whole matter (v. 35): 'Jesus heard that they had cast him out; and when He had found him, He said, Do you believe on the Son of God?' Jesus went out to look for him, went on the search for him—and found him.

It is extraordinary how three simple words can gather up into themselves and epitomise the concentrated essence of the gospel. 'Jesus found him.'

We talk so much about finding God, finding the secret of life and of an authentic existence, finding an answer to the soul's eternal quest—as though the search were all on our side, and if we did not take the initiative no one else would. But the whole New Testament declares that this is utterly mistaken. It tells that in the background all the time there is another quest going on, far surer than your quest for God or mine: God's quest for you and me. And it is a wonderful thing to realise that, whatever your longing to find God may be, it is as nothing compared with the passionate longing in God's heart to find you.

> I find, I walk, I love, but O the whole
> Of love is but my answer, Lord, to Thee;
> For Thou wast long beforehand with my soul,
> Always Thou lovedst me.

'Jesus found him'—and then comes the crowning confession and commitment: not this time 'A man called Jesus,' but from the very heart, 'Lord, I believe.' 'And he worshipped Him.'

There we must leave him, kneeling in the road before his Redeemer. I hope there are not many of us here today who will hesitate to kneel beside him. For, as we saw at the outset, we are not spectators of this or any other Gospel scene: we are all mysteriously involved in the action, participants in the drama. It is we—not some odd assortment of characters in Palestine long ago—who are at the centre of the scene with Christ. It is Christ who is at the heart of things with us. And 'Do you believe?' is still His question. Healed, forgiven, set free—do you believe? Lord, I believe. Lord, with all my heart and life I worship Thee —today, tomorrow, and for ever.

XII

WHAT IS MAN?

'Oh that men would praise the Lord for His goodness, and for His wonderful works to the children of men!'—Psalm 107:8, 15, 21, 31.

One of the beloved teachers of a former generation was that profound theologian and humble man of God, Professor Hugh R. Mackintosh. There is a sentence of his—a golden, piercing, challenging sentence—which often comes back to mind: 'I fancy that as we grow older, as we think longer and work harder and learn to sympathise more intelligently, the one thing we long to be able to pass on to men is a vast commanding sense of the grace of the Eternal. Compared with that, all else is but the small dust of the balance.'

To these words I expect that many of us here today would say Amen with all our heart. For when all is said and done—the tumult and the shouting, the theological debate and ecumenical conferring, the variations of life's experience bright and dark, the argument this way and that—there still emerges for you, for me, for all of us, the one thing needful: a vast commanding sense of the grace of the Eternal.

Now, clearly, it was to convey and communicate some such sense that this Hebrew poet wrote his psalm. Here is a man who knows how difficult life can be, the strains and stresses that our sensitive, vulnerable nature has to bear. He knows it, because he has tasted it in his own mature experience. But this also he knows, and this is the great thing he sets himself to herald and proclaim: that for every possible predicament of man there is a corresponding grace of God, for every particular human need the requisite particular supernatural resource. If this is true, then the whole world is suddenly different. And the Christian faith exists to assure us that it is literally, absolutely true. May God make us sure of it today!

Look for a moment at the structure of this poem. First comes the prologue, verses 1 to 3, a call to thanksgiving. This is followed by four main stanzas, verses 4 to 31. In these the writer has given a series of four distinct images of experience in this world, four unforgettable pictures of life's vicissitudes. You will observe that the symmetry of these four stanzas is identical. Each of them presents one distinct aspect of life, one form of the human predicament. Each then proceeds to show the decisive transformation that comes over the scene when faith lays hold on God: 'they cried unto the Lord in their trouble, and He delivered them out of their distresses'. Each leads on in the end to the same thrilling, trumpet-toned refrain: 'Oh that men would praise the Lord for His goodness, and for His wonderful works to the children of men!' Finally, the psalm closes with an epilogue, verses 32 to 43, a quiet meditation on the providential ordering of the world.

So much for structure. Now what we are going to do is this. We will lift out the four pictures here, these four characteristic images of human life, and we will ask the question—What is this saying to me about my experience? How does this apply to the actual circumstances of my life today?

Take the first stanza, the first picture, verses 4 to 9. What the poet shows us here is _Man the Pilgrim_. 'They wandered in the wilderness in a solitary way; they found no city to dwell in'—and so on. This is the image: the pilgrimage of life.

It is a picture which of course came naturally to the Jew, for the restlessness of generations of pilgrims was in his blood. Historically, his nation owed its very existence to its pilgrim fathers, Abraham and Jacob, Moses and Joshua, men without a city or a country of their own, dwelling in tents because of the dream that was driving them, homeless nomads of the desert with nowhere to lay their heads. And so this Hebrew poet, remembering that rock whence he and all his nation were hewn, takes this ancestral image, this pilgrim idea, and sets it down here, saying in effect—'Life is just like that! We are all travellers through the world, driven on by the remorseless years, making our bivouac a brief moment, and then gone.'

Only the road and the dawn, the sun, the wind, and the rain,
And the watchfire under stars, and sleep, and the road again.

This is the road which for all of us goes running through the
years, out of the east and the dawn and the lightheartedness of
youth, through the noonday and the toils of middle life, on into
the afternoon and the westering sun and the gloaming, and the
watchfire under the stars and the last encampment of all. Not a
very long road at the best: an average of three score miles and
ten, a good deal shorter for some, a little longer for others.

And it is so easy, as Bunyan reminded us, to get lost on that
pilgrimage; so terribly easy, amid the puzzling enigmas of life,
its confused and tangled complexity, its luring by-ways and
crossroads of decision, to get deflected from the true pathway
and the guiding marks of Christ.

Many who once set out gallantly in the dawn, ready to tackle
anything, have long ago lost all sense of direction in life, and
are wandering today aimless and haphazard, without any controlling or absorbing purpose; realising perhaps with a sinking
of heart that life is more than half over, and the years are not
coming back again; beginning to wonder bitterly, 'Is this all life
was meant to be—this gnawing emptiness, this meaningless perpetual frustration? How can we achieve peace and quietude and
dignity of soul amid the torturing perplexities of such a world,
or keep our outlook spiritual and serene? If you do find us
dissatisfied and cynical, or resentful and rebellious, can you be
surprised? How shall we sing the Lord's song in a strange land?'
It is precisely the picture here in the psalm. Man the pilgrim
has lost his way in the desert. 'They wandered in the wilderness.
Hungry and thirsty, their soul fainted in them.' It is no old
story, this: it is startling in its modernity.

But here the poet strikes in with the sudden transformation of
his picture. 'Then they cried unto the Lord in their trouble, and
He delivered them out of their distresses.'

For when you have said that man is a pilgrim, that is not the
whole story. He is a pilgrim *whom God can guide.* Apart from
this, our life here is indeed an aimless wandering in circles. But
what if over everything else, controlling, directing, permeating—
in the home, the factory, the shop, the school, the office—you can

be aware of a great guiding force, the hand and will of God?
What if you can actually be linked up to that force, and catch
step to its triumphant march?

> Guide me, O Thou great Jehovah,
> Pilgrim through this barren land.

It really begins to make sense then, this enigma of a life. It is
leading somewhere. It can have poise and dignity and rhythm.
Through trials and vicissitudes, it may even be through the
shattering of dreams and disciplining of heart's desire, it goes its
clear and steady way. And this is the marvellous thing about it:
the way is not just another track in the sand—it is a Person.
'I am the way,' says Jesus, 'he travels safe who journeys on with
Me.'

Man the pilgrim: yes, says the psalmist, but far more—the
pilgrim who can have God for guide. Would it not be worth
while, today and tomorrow and every day, to make time to listen
to that guiding voice? 'Oh that men would praise the Lord for
His goodness, and for His wonderful works to the children of
men!'

So we pass to the second stanza and the second picture, verses
10 to 16. Here the image is different. It is *Man the Prisoner.*
'Such as sit in darkness and the shadow of death, being bound in
affliction and iron.'

This picture also came naturally to the Jew. His fathers had
been bondslaves in the house of Egypt. They had been exiles in
the alien land of Babylon. Historically, that double bondage had
set its mark on all the Hebrew race. And so this poet, remembering again the rock whence he was hewn and the pit whence he
was digged, gives us his vivid picture of the prisoner in his
dungeon. He sets it down here, saying to us—'Life is like that!
We are all cramped in this material existence that does not give
our eternal spirits room to breathe, crushed within the suffocating
walls of circumstance too narrow for our immortality, with the
visions and dreams within us beating their wings like caged
birds against the bars of daily deadening drudgery and moral
mediocrity and all the thousand limitations from which we cannot
break free: bound in affliction and iron.'

Some there are no doubt who can live that kind of life and be quite content, not realising what they are missing; some who can be prisoners of conventionalism and conformity and secular triviality, and not really care; with no thoughts beyond a narrow, one-dimensional existence, no beckoning spiritual horizons beyond the four walls of their aimlessness and futility and agnosticism. But there are others who feel chafed intolerably, other spirits in prison who cry—'Oh God, this is dreadful! This is stifling me and killing me. I must get out! I can't go on like this. My nerves won't stand it. I must be free!' Much of the experimenting that is going on today in art and literature and morals, much of the radical and rebellious experimentation, is just this attempt to get out, away from the dead-end and the rut, out into a meaningful existence. And so often it leads only to a deeper and more racking restlessness and frustration. Certainly the psalmist was describing a great multitude when he spoke of men and women feeling crushed and cramped and miserable: 'bound in affliction and iron'.

But here he breaks in again with his sudden transforming stroke. 'Then they cried unto the Lord in their trouble, and He delivered them out of their distresses.' For when you have said that man is a prisoner, that is not all the story. He is a prisoner _whom God sets free_. Stone walls and iron bars may clamp him round; but yet he can have, even there, the glorious liberty of the children of God.

Fundamentally, the Christian faith is a message of release. But this is what so many fail to understand. Perhaps it is the Church's fault that they fail. Some run instead to new moralities and unchartered self-expressionism, sometimes to drink and drugs, the whole pathetic paraphernalia of the effort to escape. If only they knew it was all unnecessary! There is a remedy nearer at hand. For this is still God's world, full of the liberating action of the Spirit of Christ. Surely we who belong to the Church ought, by our life and conduct, to be making it clear that the faith of Christ, membership in the Body of Christ, is like the coming of a great love. It adds on another dimension to human experience. It stretches the horizons illimitably. It gives a whole new world of spiritual reality.

> Even as a bird
>> Out of the fowler's snare
> Escapes away,
>> So is our soul set free.

Man the prisoner: yes, says the psalmist, but far more—the prisoner whom God can set at liberty. How worth while to accept today, tomorrow, all the days of our life, this gift of the Spirit so freely offered! 'Oh that men would praise the Lord for His goodness, and for His wonderful works to the children of men!'

There follows the third stanza of the psalm, with the third picture, verses 17 to 22. Here again the image is different. It is *Man the Sufferer.* 'Their soul abhorreth all manner of meats; they draw near unto the gates of death.'

This picture, too, came naturally to the Jew. For in those days plague and pestilence were familiar. Perhaps the poet himself had lain on the bed of sickness which he here describes. He had known what it meant to toss sleeplessly in pain, to cry in the morning 'Would God it were evening,' and in the evening 'Would God it were morning!' He had felt in his own body the prostration of ill-health and the ravages of fever and disease. He takes that experience, and sets it down here in this picture, saying—'Life is like that! We are all poor ailing creatures. There is one malady endemic to the race. There is a scourge no soul of man escapes. It claims its victims everywhere. It is dreadfully contagious. The infection spreads. The plague stalks unchallenged through the world: the mystery of iniquity, the dilemma of collective evil, the radical corruption of man's sin.'

But is there no balm in Gilead, no physician there? If man is unhealed, it is certainly not from failure to attempt a cure, not for lack of proffered remedies. Think of the cures attempted. The balm of penance. The anaesthetic of forgetfulness. The medicine of psychological integration. The surgery of stoic asceticism. The injection of determination. The salve of ethical permissiveness. All in vain. Try eradicating sin with education, social amelioration, scientific humanism, the gallantry of a thousand high resolves: it still stubbornly refuses to yield.

But again comes the transforming stroke. 'Then they cried

unto the Lord in their trouble, and He brought them out of their distresses.' For when you have said man is sick and suffering, that is not all the story. He is a sufferer *whom God can heal.* It is worth emphasizing that this includes healing on the physical level. If we could see the history of the Christian Church in the next hundred years, might we not find the ministry of healing coming back into its own? But ultimately all healing is a derivative of reconciliation with God. And that is what the psalmist is after here. He says—'God sent His Word and healed them': which points forward to the great evangelic saying—'The Word was made flesh, and dwelt among us.' So that to the neediest amongst us Christ comes today, and says, 'O sick and ailing one, I am your health. Disintegrated and dishevelled and despairing soul, I am your healing and your life!' 'Your case may be very bad,' wrote Samuel Rutherford to some ailing souls he knew, 'but my advice is—Take you a house next door to the Physician. It will be very singular if you should prove to be the very first He ever turned away unhealed.'

Man the sufferer: yes, says the psalmist, but far more—the sufferer whom God makes whole. If this is not the gospel, what is? Surely it would be wise to accept today the great Physician's aid, the remedy Christ went to the cross to give you. 'Oh that men would praise the Lord for His goodness, and for His wonderful works to the children of men!'

There, then, are three of the psalmist's pictures: man the pilgrim, the prisoner, the sufferer. And in each case we have seen the divine addendum: the pilgrim whom God will guide; the prisoner whom God sets free; the sufferer whom God makes whole. Now come the fourth stanza and the final picture, verses 23 to 31. Here again the image is different. It is *Man the Voyager.* 'They that go down to the sea in ships, that do business in great waters'—on them the storm rises, until 'they reel to and fro and are at their wits' end'.

Once again this picture came naturally to the Jew. For the Jew dreaded the sea. The sea was the symbol of treachery. The sea was a greedy, insatiable monster devouring ships and men. So many a gallant vessel had launched out bravely into the deep, and then vanished in the trackless waste and never been heard of again. So many a voyager, travelling to some far-off shore, had never reached the haven. What tales of shipwreck and annihilation the cruel sea could tell!

The psalmist draws his picture, the most dramatic of them all, with storm winds in it and furious waves and gallantry and despair. He sets it down here and says—'Life is like that. It is a constantly hazardous adventure, this launching out into the deep. There is no certainty of making any harbour on the other side. There is no assurance of safe homecoming from the deep. Even if you survive the fierceness of the storms of life—and there is no certainty of that—can you be sure that the frail barque will round the misty promontory of death and not be wrecked for ever there? What if the desired haven of a better world is an empty dream, and the eternal dawn a myth?'

Do you remember Tennyson's Ulysses at the end of life? 'My purpose holds', he cries, 'to sail beyond the sunset'; but immediately he goes on—

> It may be that the gulfs will wash us down;
> It may be we shall touch the Happy Isles.

Always that ultimate doubt, that great misgiving. 'And ah! to know not,' complains Sir William Watson, peering into the mystery of death and the hereafter, 'to know not'—

> Whether 'tis ampler day divinelier lit
>   Or homeless night without;
> And whether, stepping forth, my soul shall see
>   New prospects, or fall sheer—a blinded thing!
> There is, O grave, thy hourly victory,
>   And there, O death, thy sting.

But for the last time comes the transforming stroke. 'Then they cried unto the Lord in their trouble, and He brought them out of their distresses.' For when you have said that man is a voyager on life's ocean, that is not all the story. He is a voyager *whom God pilots home to the harbour*. 'He bringeth them unto their desired haven.'

And that means the loved one to whom you said goodbye on

that darkest and loneliest of days that has left your life feeling blank and empty ever since. It will mean yourself one day, when the voyage ends; and there, waiting to welcome you as your ship draws in to land, that loved one of your own, waiting eager at the harbour mouth to be the first to hail you as your ship comes in, the dear one you thought lost and now have found for ever!

How do we know? It is Christ who has made us sure. 'If it were not so, I would have told you.' His revelation of God has crowned hope with certainty. His resurrection is the divine authentic guarantee. 'Because I live, ye shall live also.'

Man the voyager: yes, says the psalmist, but far more—the voyager whom God brings home. And the main part of Christian faith is just taking Jesus at His word. 'Oh that men would praise the Lord for His goodness, and for His wonderful works to the children of men!'

So the psalmist has given his four images of life, and God's transforming grace at work on each. I go back to the words I quoted at the outset. 'As we grow older,' said Hugh Mackintosh, 'the one thing we long to be able to pass on to men is a vast commanding sense of the grace of the Eternal.' If only one could pass it on to someone here and now! This at any rate is the message of that grace of the eternal: pilgrim—God can guide you; prisoner—God can release you; sufferer—God can heal you; voyager—God can bring you home. A vast commanding sense of that—is it really ours? To believe in God through Christ is to know these things are true. Surely, then, they ought to dominate our life, and exhilarate our worship, and flood our hearts with gratitude!

This psalmist of Israel seems to suggest that his people were not as consistently grateful in their response to the grace of God as they might have been; for every stanza ends with the same refrain, calling on men to praise the Lord for His wonderful works. Should we not ask ourselves what Jesus must feel about His Church's response today? Does our gratitude measure up to anything like the immense overflowing gratitude of the New Testament? I wonder if sometimes the very angels are not shocked by the stinginess of our hosannas.

We are about to sing Henry Francis Lyte's great hymn, 'Praise my soul, the King of heaven', a hymn which this psalm may well have inspired. Sometimes we sing a hymn like this cheerfully enough, because it is set to a good rousing tune, but without recapturing the essential meaning of the words, and without letting the words really bite into our consciousness. But just look at these words.

> Ransomed, healed, restored, forgiven,
> Who like me His praise should sing?

It is absolutely overwhelming, if it is true: and it is true for you, at this very moment. Look again.

> Slow to chide and swift to bless.

Slow to chide—yes, Lord, indeed, when I deserved to be blasted by a righteous anger, slow to chide, swift to bless; and like as a father pities, so the Lord has pitied me.

> Angels, help us to adore Him;
> Dwellers all in time and space.

There are dear ones yonder in the eternal glory who have reached the desired haven before us, who having loved Christ's Church on earth now behold Him face to face, and their rejoicing hallelujahs mingle with ours in one sacrifice of praise: angels helping us to adore Him. If we are ever to sing the new song in heaven, we had better be doing some practice for it now. Oh that men would praise the Lord—Oh that you and I today, ransomed, healed, restored, forgiven, with a new commanding sense of the grace of the eternal—would praise the Lord for His goodness, and for His wonderful works to the children of men!

XIII

LIFE IN A NEW DIMENSION

By the deeds of the law shall no flesh be justified ... *But now* the righteousness of God without the law is manifested—Romans 3:20, 21.

The end of those things is death. *But now* being made free from sin —Romans 6:21, 22.

At that time ye were without Christ ... aliens ... strangers ... having no hope and without God in the world. *But now* ye who were far off are made nigh by the blood of Christ—Ephesians 2:12, 13.

If in this life only we have hope in Christ, we are of all men most miserable. *But now* is Christ risen from the dead—1 Corinthians 15:19, 20.

What connects all these texts is that brief emphatic 'But now'. In each case, St. Paul has been expatiating on an age that lies behind him. In each case, he has been pointing to a different, distinctive characteristic of that bygone age. Then abruptly he changes his tone. 'That was the world we knew,' he says. 'That was typical of all our yesterdays. That was the kind of existence to which we had grown monotonously accustomed. But now everything is different. Now a new world order has arrived!'

There have been strident voices in plenty, in this maelstrom of the twentieth century, shouting to us of a new order of history. There are principalities and powers and totalitarian tyrannies trying forcibly to impose their ideology of a new order upon a browbeaten world. To this the answer of every free man rings clear: 'If that is your new order—that conscience-enslaving mechanised materialism—we refuse to go along with it. We deplore and repudiate it.'

But this is not to say that we do not feel the need of a new order ourselves. We do—emphatically. Some of those who have claimed to offer it have been wildly wrong: yet the appeal is to a true instinct of the human heart. Out of the travail and tumult of

this age there must surely emerge a juster society, an ampler life
of meaning and opportunity for all the sons of men of every race
and nation, something nearer to the mind of God and the heart
of Christ. This is a quest to which every citizen of the Kingdom
of God stands committed.

But here is St. Paul in these four passages telling us that in
one sense at least—and that the most vital of all—the new order
has already arrived. It is not a quest, it is a fact. It is not a
dream of tomorrow, it is an actuality of today. It is not yonder,
it is here. But now!

There is one of Charles Kingsley's letters where this thought
of Paul's dramatically reappears. By the way, if you want a truly
invigorating tonic when you are feeling depressed, a therapy as
bracing as a west wind, read some of Kingsley's letters. Listen to
this. 'What is our present dreariness and weariness to what it
would have been two thousand years ago? We have now'—
note the Pauline emphasis coming out—'we have now the Rock
of Ages to cling to. Then—there would have been nothing but
mist—no certainty but that of our own misery—no hope but the
stillness of death. Oh, we are highly favoured ... All is safe—
for through all time, changeless and unbroken, extends the Rock
of Ages!' And then comes a kind of irrepressible shout of praise
—'And must we not thank and thank for ever, and toil and toil
for ever for Him?'

You see the point. 'If the way be drear, if the foe be near'—
what is that dreariness compared with what it might have been?
Once it would have broken us, shattered us. But now—the Rock
of Ages to cling to!

Suppose this. Suppose the desolations that our generation has
witnessed had happened in a world where Jesus had never set
foot; suppose the rocket bomb had never been antedated by the
star of Bethlehem; suppose there had been a Hiroshima but no
Galilee, an iron curtain but no veil rent in twain from top to
bottom—we might well at this moment have been plunged in
pessimism and despair. Yes, indeed. But now!

Or again, suppose this. Suppose your sins and mine were to
stand accusing us at the bar of conscience, and we could not—in
John Newton's words—'face that fierce accuser and tell him
Christ has died'; suppose there were no crucified Lamb of God

taking our sin upon Himself and crying 'Father, forgive them'; suppose every mistake were irreparable and there were no message of a new beginning—can you imagine the midnight of our misery? But now!

Or once again, suppose that on the day when you lost a dear one, and had to follow the slow procession to the grave, you had never heard of the Easter garden and the shattering of the midnight by the light from an empty tomb, and the communion of saints and the swallowing up of death in victory—how desolate the world, how inconsolable your grief! Yes, indeed. But now!

Something has happened, says Paul. Something tremendous has got a foothold on this darkened scene, something that changes the face of the world for ever, and makes it wonderful to be alive!

Such is the biblical insight. Do we share it? Some would doubtless say—'Sheer exaggeration, the emotional hyperbole of a religious fanaticism! Look at the world. Wonderful to be alive? In a tumultuous, violent, refractory age like this? What is the sense of talking about a heavenly kingdom and a conquering Christ in this Babylonian chaos of a world? The only true philosopher is the cynic!'

Even Christians are not entirely immune from some shadow of doubt. One of the disquieting things about church life today is the number of Christian people who are just as pessimistic about the world as any unbeliever, just as defeatist about the human prospect. We all have moods when doubt inhibits faith. 'He came unto His own, and His own received Him not.'

But that is the very spirit to which Paul, in a far grimmer age than ours, rings out his magnificent trumpet-toned rejoinder. 'Yes —all that may have been inevitable once, that heavy pessimism, frighteningly and inescapably inevitable. But now! Now the darkness has been routed, the vicious circle broken, and God is on the field when He is most invisible!'

This means that now, this very moment, we can be living a new quality of life, with the dimension of eternity in it. For we belong, not to the old hopeless treadmill of man's irreparable pilgrimage towards disillusionment, but to a new exciting era, the era God launched into history when He gave us Christ. Once sorrow, sin, corruption, death had the last word with the hopes of humanity. But now! Now above the flood-line stands the Rock of Ages, the mightiest of all the mighty acts of God.

In these four texts, Paul is trying to help us grasp the reality and personal significance of this new era that has broken in upon us. He gives four distinct descriptions of it—four reasons why it is wonderful to be alive today.

First, this: it is wonderful to be alive, because in Christ *something has happened to man's struggle*. 'By the deeds of the law,' he writes to the Romans, 'shall no flesh be justified ... But now the righteousness of God without the law is manifested.'

'By the deeds of the law'—that means, by the old method of struggling to keep the commandments. By labouring grimly at the cultivation of character. By trying to build a new world from beneath. By adopting a creed of scientific self-salvation. By imagining we can eliminate the corporate evils of the body politic by better social planning, or fight down temptation by naked resolution, suppressing our own particular private devil by main force. It is a gallant and heroic warfare, no doubt: but it is not the gospel.

There is a moving moment in Scott's *Ivanhoe*, where Rebecca is facing her most difficult renunciation. 'I will tear this affection from my heart,' she cries, 'though every fibre bleed as I rend it away.' Noble, indeed. We bow before the nobility of such a spirit. But is that the best? On the battlefields where men struggle for their souls and for the soul of the world, is there no better way? Are we thrust back upon the resources of a stoic resolution? Is the world, seeking salvation, thrown back on man's ethical energies? A heartbreaking business. 'By the deeds of the law shall no flesh be justified.' That way lies only disenchantment and defeat.

But now! Now in Christ the new dynamic has appeared. Now there are incalculable resources for the fight. Surely the most wrong-headed psychology in the world is that which speaks of you and me as closed personalities, with just so much strength and no more, with strictly limited reserves of power. For what Christ has done is to make us feel, at all the gateways of our nature, the pressure and bombardment of the infinite energies of a world unseen. He has shown us how our little life, with unsearchable riches to draw on, can be reinforced beyond all calculation. I may not be able to fight down some evil thing. But if Christ were here, He could. So then, if Christ is in me, in me He can. This transfusion of spirit and energy is really possible. If Shakespeare were in you, what poetry you could write! If Mozart were in you, what music you could make! That cannot be. But here is something that can: if Christ were in you, what a life you could live! This is faith's logic. God wants you to know you can rise above the level of your limitations. 'I can do all things through Christ who strengtheneth me.'

This, then, is Paul's first description of the new order, his first characteristic 'But now!' It is wonderful to be alive, because something has happened to man's struggle.

But he goes further. It is wonderful to be alive because *something has happened to man's sin*. 'You were the slaves of sin,' he writes again to the Romans, 'and the end of those things is death. But now being made free from sin.'

Paul knew, you see, it is not enough to be reinforced for our present struggle: we want also reassurance about the past defeat. When sin has once come upon the scene and evil has taken the game into its hateful hands, when things have happened and left a mark and wrought themselves indelibly into the texture of social, international or individual life, you cannot just dismiss it by a process of ignoring or suppression. You cannot pacify the guilty conscience of a whole generation or a single soul by saying to it—'Don't worry! To err is human, to sin is universal. Put those disturbing thoughts away!' Will that sham comfort sophisticate the soul into believing that the past, being done, is also done with? Man knows better. The coiled chain of his guilt holds him in relentless grasp: and the end of those things is death. No one ever knew this better than Paul himself. 'O wretched man that I am! Who shall deliver me?' He had stared that grim destiny in the face: 'never glad confident morning again'.

'But now!' he cries. Now the hands once pierced on Calvary have torn that chain of the past away. Now the indelible stain is obliterated by the forgiveness of God.

I beg you not to think of this word forgiveness as a remote theological abstraction. It is anything but that. It is the living

Christ coming to one and another in this church today, using the most intimate personal form of address, and saying—'Be of good cheer! I have come to tell you God is at peace with you. The shadow is gone, the barrier finished now for ever.' What can you do, hearing that, but arise and shine, knowing that the darkness is routed and the night gone, and the glory of the Lord risen upon you?

> O loving wisdom of our God!
> When all was sin and shame,
> A second Adam to the fight
> And to the rescue came.

Once—no hope at all. But now! 'I will take the cup of salvation, and call upon the name of the Lord.'

But Paul's characterisation of the new order goes further. It is wonderful to be alive, because *something has happened to man's solitude and segregation.* This is the theme of the vivid words in which he describes to the Ephesians their former isolation as Gentiles and outsiders, racially discriminated against, and remote from the main track of God's historic redemption: 'At that time you were without Christ, aliens from the commonwealth of Israel, strangers from the covenants of promise, having no hope, and without God in the world'—the very words are heavy with a desolating sense of solitude and forsakenness—'but now in Christ Jesus you who were far off are made nigh by the blood of Christ.'

Now it is the personal meaning of this that we are after. But here it has to be emphasized that on the wider scale of civilisation these words must mean sooner or later the end of racial segregation. You who were afar off, you disinherited ones shut out by pride of privilege into racial solitude and isolation, you have been brought right into the fellowship of the great Father's care. Once men called you Gentiles, inferior members of the family, lesser breeds without the law, aliens, strangers, existing to be exploited. But now! Now the last are becoming the first, the furthest off the nearest to the throne of grace. Now there is to be one Lord, one faith, one baptism, one ransomed family of Christ.

That is why we take our holy faith out into all the world. That is why an institution that was not missionary would be a caricature of Christ's intention. That is why the Church is having to declare the perpetuation of barriers, the discrimination that denies human rights, to be an affront to the universal Fatherhood of God. If the gospel of Christ means anything, it means that once there was a wall of partition, but that now the wall is down for ever, the aliens full citizens of Jerusalem. 'Write down his name,' cries the poet of the eighty-seventh psalm, 'this man was born in Zion!' And to filch away those title-deeds is a crime.

That on the wider scale. But take it on the scale of the individual. There are lonely folk in this church today. There are solitary souls wherever a congregation meets. There are lonely moods for everyone. And one of the terrifying things in life is solitude. It is a grim kind of starvation—the famine for fellow-ship. People don't always tell you: they are too brave to complain. But often the secret cry is—'Why does no one understand? Why are there so many harsh exclusions in this world? Why this sense of being shut out, unwanted, unbefriended?' It is a destiny that multitudes know. And when Paul talks here about aliens, men without a home, strangers from the covenants, there are so many who understand all too well what he means, and would say—'Yes, that is my own experience mirrored exactly!'

> O Wedding-Guest! this soul hath been
> Alone on a wide wide sea;
> So lonely 'twas, that God Himself
> Scarce seemed there to be.

That once—perhaps for years on end. But now! Now in Christ the isolation is ended. 'You who were afar off are made nigh.' On the authority of Christ I am to speak to the loneliest soul in this church today, and say—'Friend, He has brought you to His banqueting-house, and His banner over you is love.' Yours is to be this most intimate personal communion, your name inscribed in the Lamb's book of life. The wilderness and the solitary place shall be glad for you, and the desert blossom as the rose. Perhaps you can even feel the tide of the charity of Christ beginning to sweep up around you now from the fellowship of a Christian congregation. This is Christ's new order, yours to inherit for ever.

Now comes Paul's final characterisation of the new era. It is wonderful to be alive, because *something has happened to man's setting sun*. Paul's words on this are worthy of his theme. 'If in this life only we have hope in Christ, we are of all men most miserable.' If there is nothing beyond the sunset and the gloaming and the dark, if death is a sleep from which there is no awaking, then all our pilgrimage here is purposeless and intolerably pathetic, as pathetic as a funeral bell. 'Do not send,' cried John Donne in the pulpit of St. Paul's, 'to enquire for whom the bell tolls—it tolls for thee!' One—two—three—and doom in every chime. All this—once. 'But now,' and with these words the apostle sets the resurrection trumpet to his lips, 'now is Christ risen from the dead!'

Ring out, wild bells, to the wild sky,
Ring in the Christ that is to be.

'Now is Christ risen, the first fruits of them that slept.'

Something has happened to man's setting sun. 'Christ,' said Clement of Alexandria magnificently, 'has turned all our sunsets into dawns.'

That is why the people of God can face the last enemy without a tremor, and the true believer walks unshaken and serene. Once —death could have been the crash and ruin of our hopes. It could have been a field mocking our mortality. 'Sunset and evening star' could have been sheer tragedy. 'Death,' said Aristotle, 'is a fearful thing, for it is the end.' Yes, once—but now! Now is Christ risen. Now death is ultimately irrelevant. Now sunset floods the whole horizon with the promise of resurrection dawn.

There was a Scottish Covenanting martyr who hailed the morning of his execution with the psalmist's cry: 'This is the day which the Lord hath made; we will rejoice and be glad in it.' And he went forth singing to his death. This is the victory. Once the days of our life were three score years and ten, and after that the darkness of an endless night. But now—how exhilaratingly different!

The King there in His beauty
  Without a veil is seen;
It were a well-spent journey
  Though seven deaths lay between.
The Lamb with His fair army
  Doth on Mount Zion stand;
And glory, glory dwelleth
  In Immanuel's land.

It may be that this is an hour of decision for someone here, an hour of reaffirmation for another. You will never regret yielding yourself to this Christ who has promised to be with you in your struggle and your sin, your solitude and your setting sun. His first coming inaugurated God's new order for the world. His daily renewed coming still brings an era of hope and victory and serenity for all who welcome Him in faith. 'As many as received Him, to them gave He power to become the sons of God.' Will you take Him at His word? The past is past. But now —the Christ who is to be!

XIV

THE LOVE OF THE FORGIVEN

'Jesus saith to Simon Peter, Simon, son of Jonas, lovest thou Me more than these? He saith unto Him, Yea, Lord; Thou knowest that I love Thee. He saith unto him, Feed My lambs'—John 21:15.

It is a very moving fact that this scene, the closing scene in the long drama of Jesus' dealings with His disciples, is cast at the same spot where the first scene of all had been enacted—on the shores of the Lake of Galilee. The wheel has gone full circle, and they are back where they began.

It is always a moving experience—to go back after absence to a place of many memories: to stand again on the ground where you dreamed the dreams of youth, or awoke to the beauty of literature, nature, music, or fell in love, or stood beside a parent's grave, or met the Saviour of your soul. This going back touches chords of strange emotion. We Scots know something about that. We understand vividly what our own dear poet meant who cried—

> Sing me a song of a lad that is gone,
>   Say, could that lad be I? ...
> Give me again all that was there,
>   Give me the sun that shone!
> Give me the eyes, give me the soul,
>   Give me the lad that's gone!

These are 'thoughts that lie too deep for tears'.

So it was here: this last scene in the Gospel is laid where the first had taken place. There is more in this than meets the eye. Here was Peter, back in the old fishing-boat, at the old occupation and the old life. Here was the man who had risen up and left it, that spring morning when Jesus had come and called him, left it—as he had thought then—for good and all; here he was taking it up again, almost as though those other years had never intervened. Here is the laconic remark: 'I go a-fishing.' We want to know why. What was in Peter's mind?

You have only to read between the lines to find the answer. As clearly as any words could say it, Peter's reversion to the old fisherman life meant: 'The other adventure, the Christ adventure, is finished. Christ may be risen from the dead, and others may go and follow Him; but for me the dream is over. I had my chance, a glorious chance—and I broke my troth and disowned Him, swore I never knew Him. I vowed I could play the hero more than all these others, and I have been the worst of cowards. Three times over it happened, the beastly thing; once, twice, thrice I trampled Christ's beloved name beneath my feet. I am not fit for the Kingdom of God. I had best go back where I came from: it is all I am good for now. I go a-fishing!'

And some of the others, realising that they too had failed most lamentably, joined him. 'We also go with thee.'

> I am battered and broken and weary and out of heart,
> I will not hear of talk of heroic things,
> But be content to play some simple part,
> Freed from preposterous, wild imaginings:
> Men were not meant to walk as priests and kings.

Back at the old life! But it was not an auspicious return. 'That night they caught nothing.' And I think that all through the hours of darkness Peter's thoughts must have kept flying back to another occasion, another night on the same fishing-ground. He was remembering the last time he had sailed his boat on the highland loch three years before, and how that night also they had caught nothing; and how in the morning twilight Someone had stood on the shore and called him to become a fisher of men. So piercing was the memory that it was almost as if time turned back in its flight: almost he could fancy it was still that wonderful daybreak three years ago, almost he could see Jesus standing there and hear that blessed voice calling him. Never surely had there been a dawn like that since the making of the world! But suddenly he awoke from the reverie and the happy dream; and back came rushing upon him the bitter, sad reality of the present,

This narrative evokes many emotional thoughts & memories. Excellent setting of the scene

and all the cold, clammy misery of the thought—'I've lost that lovely dream for ever, and all the splendour of the dawn is shattered beyond recall.'

> Billow and breeze, islands and seas,
> Mountains of rain and sun,
> All that was good, all that was fair,
> All that was me is gone.

'But if only it could come back again! If only it were not a dream, but real and true and here! How I should leap to it this time, if the chance were mine! Too late, Simon son of Jonas, too late. Never again! Never again.'

Suddenly at that moment there was a rough hand on his shoulder. And Peter looked up. It was John, shaking him, and pointing. 'Look, Peter, yonder—look!' There was a strange excitement in his voice. Peter followed that pointing finger, and through the trailing mists saw Someone on the shore. 'Well, what about it?' he asked. 'What's all your flurry?' 'But, man,' cried John, 'are you blind? Don't you see who it is? You must see. It is the Lord!' And Peter shaded his eyes, and looked again. And suddenly he understood. 'O God, then it was not a dream after all! It has miraculously come true. It is indeed happening all over again!' And the next hour was worth a lifetime—the leaping into the sea, the encounter on the beach, the meal around the fire; and then somehow, quite suddenly, Peter finding himself alone with Jesus, with the others at a little distance and just the Master and himself together; and then the question on the Saviour's lips—'Simon, son of Jonas, lovest thou Me more than these?'

Here, then, is this gleaming and immortal scrap of dialogue between Jesus and Peter. Notice that there are three things in it: a challenge, a confession, a commission. And the significant thing is that you have each of them three times over. There is the challenge, thrice repeated: 'Lovest thou Me?' There is the confession, thrice repeated: 'Thou knowest that I love Thee.' There is the commission, thrice repeated: 'Feed My sheep.' Let us look into this, and see what it has to say to us.

First, *the challenge*. 'Simon, son of Jonas, lovest thou Me? Do you love Me, Peter, more than these others do?'

Can you guess why Jesus said it thrice? Would not once have been enough? Why the reiteration? The evangelist records that, at the third time of asking, Peter was vexed and grieved that Christ should think this necessary. And perhaps you say, 'No wonder! He was entitled to be vexed. I should have felt Christ did not trust me.'

But look again. May it not be that this is the symbolism of the divine forgiveness? For there had been three denials. Three times over on the night of shame Peter had declared 'I know not the Man'. Three times he had struck that poisoned dagger at the heart of love. So what was happening here was that God was providing for that triple sin a triple obliteration. Thrice let this three times pardoned disciple tell out his love!

'Simon, son of Jonas, who promised that if all the world forsook Me you would stand beside Me to the end, do you now love Me more than these others? Simon, son of Jonas, do you love Me? Simon, son of Jonas, are you My friend?'

Now there are three things to notice about that question. First, it was *a simple question*. In fact, this is Christ's great simplification of religion. He did not say—though well He might—'Simon, are you ashamed and contrite and ready to do penance?' He did not say, 'Simon, are you sure now of the stability of your faith, and confident of the complexities of your creed?' He might have spoken thus. But with one stroke He cut right down to the heart of the matter: 'Simon, son of Jonas, do you love Me?'

This is our Lord's breath-taking simplification of religion. It all comes down to this at last: Do you love Christ? I used to try to make this clear to my young communicants when they came forward to be confirmed and to join the Church. I tried to tell them that the real question was not 'Have you got all the answers to the problems of creed and conduct?' not 'Are you satisfied you understand the doctrines of election and creation and the Trinity?'—that the real question was: 'Recognising that this Jesus is the highest you will ever see on earth, do you love the highest when you see it?'

Perhaps within the organised Church we are rather frightened of this note today. There are areas of our institutional Christianity which have a notable tradition of devotion to the truth, of patient intellectual quest, of the discipline of building up the faith into a firm philosophy. And that is great gain. We need the dialectic of faith. But is there never a danger that we may over-intellectualise our religion? There is a Scottish Paraphrase which declares that when the Holy Spirit comes He does two things, not one:

> Your minds shall fill with sacred truth,
> Your hearts with sacred fire.

Sometimes the Church has been so keen about the first, the quest of sacred truth, that it has rather tended to play down the second, the sacred fire of love. And when that happens, you are bound to get a Church inhibited and crippled, lacking verve and glow and warmth and spontaneity. 'I baptise you with water,' declared John the Baptist, 'but He shall baptise you with fire.' 'Let your religion,' cried G. K. Chesterton impatiently, 'be less of a theory and more of a love affair!' There was a day when Father Stanton, in his pulpit of St. Alban's, Holborn, suddenly cried 'Fire! Fire!'—and then when the congregation was beginning to panic, he went on 'Everywhere, everywhere—except in the Church!' Do let us remember that what the gospel gives is not a problem but a Person; not an -ism or an -ology, but the Word made flesh; not a metaphysic but a master-passion, a living Lord to love and to be loved by for ever. 'Simon, son of Jonas, lovest thou Me?'

It was a simple question. But it was also *a searching question,* a terribly probing question. What short work this question makes of all our shams and sophistries and insincerities!

There was once a Russian artist who painted a picture of the Last Supper. When it was finished, being rather pleased with it, he took it to Tolstoy and said, 'I want your opinion of my picture: what do you think of my Christ?' And Tolstoy, having looked carefully at the picture, turned round with blazing eyes on the artist, and in a voice trembling with emotion exclaimed 'You don't love Him! For if you did, you would have painted Him better. And if you don't love Him, what right have you to touch Him at all?'

A simple question, a searching question—and, above all, *a*

saving question. For it was the dynamic of Christ's redeeming
love and patience that pursued Peter back to the old boat on the
old loch, tracked him down in the dawning and carried the question deep into the ruins of his shamed and broken heart. In
Robert Browning's *The Ring and the Book* the dying Pompilia
is speaking about the brutal husband who had wrecked her life:
'I could not love him,' she cries, 'but—his mother did!' Here
was Peter, feeling himself to be the most unlovable creature in
God's universe. 'No one could possibly love me now. But—
Jesus did!' And that is salvation.

'Lovest thou Me?'—a simple, searching, saving question. And
if anyone objects, 'No, to me it sounds sentimental! It is pander-
ing to the weak emotionalism of an individualist religion devoid
of social passion'—then, my friend, hating sentimentality in
religion as I do, I must listen to you. But my answer is that
'sentimental' is the one thing it is not. For it involves decision. It
means, not aesthetic enjoyment, but the courage of heroic action.
It means something like the ancient word of Elijah on Mount
Carmel, ringing like a thousand trumpets across the darkness:
'How long go ye halting between two opinions?' That surely is
the weak and flabby thing, that hybrid, amphibian existence lacking the courage to decide. 'How long go ye limping between the
two sides? If Jehovah be God, follow Him; but if Baal, then
follow him.' Weak? Sentimental—this 'Lovest thou Me'? Why,
men have been burnt to ashes in its flames. Yes, and it has held
men poised, erect and sane amid the madness of the world. And
if that Christ, with that question, should come over the horizon
of some confused, bewildered soul today, then, Simon, son of
Jonas, look up, and lift up your head, for your redemption has
come nigh!

We have seen, then, the threefold Challenge. We turn now to
the threefold *Confession*. 'Lovest thou Me more than these?'
Peter answered, 'Yea, Lord, Thou knowest that I love Thee.'

It is perhaps significant that in the Greek the word for 'love'
here is different. It might in fact be translated, 'Thou knowest
I am Thy friend.' It is as though Peter would hardly dare to use
Jesus' word, which meant love pure, stainless, unsullied.

But at any rate the point is this. Here was Peter, wanting to prove his love for Jesus. To what could he appeal, to prove it? He could not appeal to his own record: that was smirched with shame. He could not appeal to his reputation as a man of his word: that reputation was gone. He could not appeal to the witness of his fellow-disciples: they had seen him play the coward. He had nothing, absolutely nothing, to appeal to, nothing to prove his love was genuine.

And yet—was there nothing? One thing surely was left him, and in a flash he saw it. Of course! The understanding heart of Jesus Himself! 'I will appeal to that.' And he did. 'Lord, You know all things. You know the whole story, all the atrocious colossal shame of my defeat. And You know that, in spite of everything, I love You still!'

Can you and I not fall back on that? Spurgeon used to tell of a poor bedridden woman whose faith, once bright, had gone under a cloud and suffered total eclipse. One day when he was visiting her, 'I don't think,' she said to him, 'that I have any real faith left nowadays or any true love to Christ whatever.' But he was a wise man. He did not argue with her. He took a piece of paper, and walked to the window and wrote the words 'I do not love the Lord Jesus Christ.' Then he brought it back, with a pencil, and said 'Now, my dear friend, you just sign that.' She took it, and read it. 'I can't sign that,' she cried. 'It's not true! I'd be torn in pieces before I'd sign that.' 'But you said it just now,' he answered, 'you know you said it.' 'Ah, but I could not put my hand to it,' she answered. 'Well then,' he went on, 'I suspect you do love Him after all.' 'Yes, yes,' she cried, 'I see it now! I do love Him—Christ knows I love Him!'

Cannot you and I, when every other appeal or proof is gone, fall back on that—the understanding heart of Jesus? 'Thou knowest that I love Thee!' Though there is absolutely nothing to show for it and all the outward evidence is dead against it, though time and again my most confident professions have crashed in ruin, though I have hurt You, disappointed You, flouted You, sinned away my very right to talk of loving You— yet, Lord, You who understand the whole story, You know I love You still!

Othello, in the play, out of his confusion and bewilderment cries to his Desdemona—'But I do love thee! And when I love thee not, chaos is come again.' This is the sinner's plea to Christ, when every other plea is gone. As Principal James Denney used to put it—'The one thing that makes me even the kind of Christian that I am is that I dare not turn my back on Christ and put Him out of my life.' 'Lord, Thou knowest all things: Thou knowest that I love Thee.'

The threefold Challenge, and the threefold Confession—and now, finally, the threefold *Commission*. Jesus said to Peter, 'Feed My lambs. Shepherd My sheep!'

Do you see what was happening? In this commission Jesus was doing two things: He was trusting the man, and He was testing him.

Trusting him—for here was Christ, so soon to leave the world and return to the Father, arranging for the future of His work by putting it all into the hands of this disciple who had failed Him so notoriously. 'You, Peter, I make the shepherd of My flock.'

Any angel, looking out from heaven at that moment, might well have cried—'No, Jesus, You are blundering! You are taking a risk You have no right to take. For that man You are confiding in—he is the least dependable of all God's creatures. To trust that man is folly!'

But three times over Jesus said it: 'Shepherd My sheep.' Three times—so that there could be no shadow of doubt—proclaiming His utter confidence in Peter.

Folly? Yes, indeed. Arrant folly! But—the folly of God: that superb, fantastic risk without which there would have been no gospel at all. St. Paul called it 'the foolishness of God' which is 'wiser than men'. Of course, the sane and prudent world would have said—as it often says today—'Don't trust that man! Don't let him imagine you trust him. Or if you must take him on again, give him a thoroughly subordinate place, a hired servant, not a son.' That is the world's way, entirely fair—and entirely futile.

But Christ's way and God's way? That is how souls are made. Look at Peter, listening to that amazing commission from his Master's lips, trying in a bewildered way to realise it—'He is saying this to me, the breaker of faith, the worthless earthen vessel, the man without a hope. To me! I am to be trusted again, given this commission far surpassing what I had before. What does it mean?' And then suddenly he saw it. 'If He cares for me like this, cares enough to trust me with a trust so royal, why then—here stand I! I can no other. From this moment, I stand up and live; and I vow to heaven that never will I fail Him again —never, never—so help me God! And in death may I behold His face in glory.'

Nor did he fail. This Fourth Gospel leads on to the Acts of the Apostles. Look at Peter of the Book of Acts, Peter of the day of Pentecost and of the early Church, defying Annas and Caiaphas and all their tribe, Peter who died at last on a cross in Rome. What a resolute, glorious rock of a man! And all because here, on this specific day, the Lord had trusted him so.

Indeed the folly of God is wiser than men. And that is how saints are made.

And to anyone who has come into this church today burdened and unhappy, the word of the Lord is this: Christ is trusting you. After everything and in spite of everything, with all His heart He is trusting you.

This is Christ's revenge for the wrongs we have done Him, His only revenge—to trust us more than ever. What can you do, trusted like that, but stand up a new man, with a new heart and a new resolve, and a new passion for His service?

> O, never let me wound again
> The love that set me free,
> Nor ever crucify afresh
> The God who died for me!

'Feed My sheep.' Christ was trusting Peter. He was also testing him. For the only way to prove love is by serving the men and women for whom Christ died.

This is the test. Any evangelicalism that stops short of this is a travesty of the truth. Any self-centred Jesus-worship is an utter contradiction. Any Church that goes on repeating 'Lord, Lord,' and yet is censorious of the world's confusion and aloof from its harrowing plight, content to exist as an exclusive spiritual coterie concerned only to maintain its own life, is earning Jesus' final rebuke—'Depart from Me! I know you not.'

Some time ago I had a letter from a young missionary on his first arrival in India to serve Christ's Church and Kingdom there. He said that his first impression of India, the thing that smote him in the face, was the appalling poverty and suffering everywhere, all those thousands who sleep out at nights in the streets because they have no homes, those tens of thousands emaciated by disease through malnutrition. Reading that letter, I remembered something in the Gospels. Jesus told a parable about a rich man who fared sumptuously every day, and a poor beggar full of sores who lay at his gate, waiting for crumbs from the rich man's table. It was not because Dives was a bad man that he ended up in torment. It was just because he never seemed to notice Lazarus at the gate, or if he did notice felt it was not his concern.

That is our world today: this privileged western civilisation, this façade of the affluent society, this fully organised western Church—and the Lazarus at our gates, the great underprivileged multitude, the world, the needy, starving, sinful, unbelieving world of which the gospel says God loved it so much that He gave His Son to die for it, and of which Jesus in the parable declares that the test of our love for God is our awareness of that world outside. This is the gospel—'God so loved the world', the suffering, despairing, unconverted world. And if that is the gospel, what right have we to call ourselves gospel Christians unless we are breaking down every ecclesiastical fence round our love to Christ, and identifying ourselves with the lost and lonely world for which He died? This is the test: and it is here, as the parable makes clear, that our own spiritual destiny, our final destination, is going to be decided. 'When the evening of this life comes,' said St. John of the Cross, 'we shall be judged on love.' Feed My lambs. Shepherd My scattered sheep. And inasmuch as you do it to one of the least of these, you do it unto Christ.

XV

EXPECT GREAT THINGS FROM GOD

For a church anniversary

'[Jesus said,] Father, glorify Thy name. Then came there a voice from heaven, saying, I have both glorified it, and will glorify it again' —John 12:28.

These words are a dramatic assertion of one basic fact of our faith: the fact, namely, that it is God's way to go beyond the best He has done before; that therefore a living faith will always have in it a certain element of surprise and tension and discovery; that what we have seen and learned of God up to the present is not to be the end of our seeing nor the sum total of our learning; that whatever we have found in Christ is only a fraction of what we still can find; that the spiritual force which in the great days of the past vitalised the Church and shaped the course of history has not exhausted its energies and fallen into abeyance but is liable at any moment to burst out anew and take control; and that specially today, when you are celebrating the anniversary of your Congregation, God is promising to do wonders for you that He has never done before, so that there will be more jubilant doxologies, more exultant hallelujahs. 'I have both glorified My name, and will glorify it again.' It is the truth we sing in Whittier's hymn:

> Immortal Love, for ever full,
> For ever flowing free,
> For ever shared, for ever whole,
> A never-ebbing sea!

For there is no limit to the creative love of God, and no end to the redeeming grace of Christ.

It is immensely important, in these difficult and sometimes discouraging days, that we should get this clear and realise what is at stake. But first it is necessary, before enquiring what these words may mean for ourselves and for the life of our Church, to try to see what they must have meant in the experience of Jesus, to whom they were originally spoken.

Here was Jesus with Galilee behind Him and Jerusalem and the cross in front of Him. The appointed hour had come. 'Father, glorify Thy name.' This was His prayer. In these words He was offering Himself, at whatever cost, to fulfil God's uttermost will, so that the revelation of the divine character and saving purpose should be crowned and made complete. 'Glorify Thy name.' Then there came a voice from heaven saying, 'I have both glorified it, and will glorify it again.'

'I have glorified it.' What did that signify? Surely the whole Galilean ministry. The total activity of Jesus up to this point was included here: in every word He had spoken and every deed He had done, God had been glorifying His name. All the compassion that had healed the sick, the pity that had fed the hungry, the love that had cheered the lonely, the mercy that had sought the sinful, the power that had broken the fetters and shackles of habit and set the prisoners free; all the grace that had availed for Peter, for Zacchaeus, for Matthew, for Mary Magdalene, for a host of others—all this had been God glorifying His name, showing forth through Jesus the very nature and character of the eternal. Probably we ought to see in these words a reference to one mighty deed in particular which had outshone the rest—it is referred to significantly throughout this chapter—the raising of Lazarus. For on that day the Lord had faced man's last grim enemy, and had trampled the pomp of death beneath His feet. 'Lazarus, come forth!' And the dead had stood up and lived. And now here at the end God says, 'I have glorified My name.' Yes, indeed it was true. More visibly than anywhere else in history, God had glorified His name in all those shining mighty works of Jesus.

'Therefore,' went on the voice, 'My beloved Son, be of good courage. I have glorified it—and will glorify it again: glorify it by a greater death and resurrection than that of Lazarus, glorify it by a mightier deed than the stilling of the storm or the feeding of the multitude, glorify it by a salvation that will reach out beyond the narrow limits of the land of Jewry and the lost sheep of the house of Israel to embrace all nations of mankind, a gospel that will outlast the stars and stand towering over the wrecks of time for ever. I have glorified it, these past short years in Galilee; and now supremely, I am about to glorify it again!' And we read that Jesus, strengthened by the voice of heaven, went forth to His last conflict like a conqueror.

It is something like this that the words of our text must have meant in the experience of Jesus. We are going on to ask, What may they mean for the Church today? In particular, what is the word of the Lord here for this Congregation at the milestone of its anniversary?

But perhaps there is a prior question to ask in passing. What of the realm of personal providence? Is there not something in our text to illuminate the ways of providence with our individual lives?

'I have glorified My name.' Can you not say, looking back today along the road you have travelled, that God has indeed been doing this very thing in your life's history? Robert Browning once, voyaging in sight of Trafalgar and Cape Saint Vincent and Gibraltar, illustrious and historic names, found himself crying, 'Here and here did England help me: how can I help England?' And you today, recalling the course of your own voyage of life, and seeing certain decisive experiences standing out behind you like headlands in the sun, can say—'Here, and here, and here did God help me! Here was the divinity that shapes our ends. Here was the providence that plans and guides our way. Here was God glorifying His name in me!'

There were perhaps dark days which you could never have struggled through, if God had not been there at your right hand. There were joys so shining and so splendid that you knew at once they came to you straight out of heaven. To mention only one, there is the love of husband and wife. 'There is no surprise more magical,' wrote Charles Morgan the novelist, 'than the surprise of being loved. It is the finger of God on a man's shoulder.' There were trials and troubles that might have left you hard and disillusioned and cynical and embittered, ready to blow out recklessly the lights of faith, if Jesus had not laid His hand upon you, just as He did upon so many ailing, fevered folk in Galilee, and saved you by His grace. 'I have glorified My name': you know of a truth that God has done this very thing for you.

Why, then, doubt the future? 'I have both glorified it, and will glorify it again'—throughout all your experience on the yet untravelled way.

And if you say, 'But life is so uncertain, and all my calculable security so precarious; and time runs so fast, and opportunities vanish never to return; and health snaps, and plans fail, and dear ones die, and never morning wears to evening but some heart must break; and even for me, at any moment some sudden crashing dispensation of trouble may break in to wreck and ruin the whole pattern and structure of my hopes'—if you feel inclined to argue thus, do stop and think! Is there any point in your past experience of which you can say, 'God failed me there'? Be honest about this. Call to mind, if you will, the darkest and most shattering sorrow you have ever had. I challenge you to look up into the face of heaven and say, 'Lord God, You failed me there!' You know you cannot do that. For was it not precisely there in the darkest valley that you proved how all-sufficient is His grace? St. Augustine said a marvellous thing about the love of God in Christ. *Non amat et deserit*: He does not love and desert. Has He not promised to be with you right on to the Judgment seat and beyond? Expect great things from God!

> Your harps, ye trembling saints,
> Down from the willows take:
> Loud to the praise of love divine
> Bid every string awake.

'I have glorified My name in you—and will glorify it again.' O Lord of hosts, blessed is the man who trusts in Thee!

But now, what of the Church? What do the words of our text signify for the Church of our own land and of all the world?

There have been periods in history when the Church has been content to live in the past, tending the fires on the altars of memory, and nostalgically harking back to the great flood-tide days of spiritual power and revival. What happens? That kind of Church, concerned as it may be to preserve the vision from the touch of time and the menace of decay, comes to be characterised by rigidity, inflexibility, loss of vitality and vigour. It is settled, static, unproductive, without dynamic contagion or living enthusiasm, suffering from a hardening of the arteries of its spirit, entrenched in traditions irrelevant to an age of revolutionary secularism, and finally paralysed into immobility.

But turn to the New Testament, and you find a religion and a Church totally different. Here all is freshness and wonder, and a strange eager tension of expectancy, and the continual surprise of discovery. These men indeed had behind them a mighty experience and a memorable hour. But they were not living in a past however sacred. Had not Jesus promised, 'Greater things than these shall ye see'? Had not God declared, 'I have glorified My name, and will glorify it again'? And was not this the thrill, the inexpressible excitement, of being alive in the same world with the risen Christ—that you just had to keep your eyes open and your soul on tiptoe, for at any moment some new startling discovery might come breaking in, some fresh unheard-of revelation to leave you lost in wonder, love and praise? The whole Church was then expecting great things from God.

Now this is characteristic Christianity. This is what God intends His Church to be—not a static camp, but a marching army; not the arrested development of an introverted fellowship which, having a certain amount of religious tradition in the background, blindly imagines that there is nothing more to find and no more land to be possessed—as though Christ's were 'the touch of a vanished hand, and the sound of a voice that is still'; not that—but a host on pilgrimage, with the certainty, the glorious humbling certainty, that they are only on the edge and outskirts of God's immeasurable grace, and that always there are new insights to achieve, new wonders to explore, new depths of the unsearchable riches to fathom.

What is the most urgent necessity for the Church today? Not surely—as some would have it—the replacing of the image of a Father in heaven with some metaphysical abstraction about the ground of being. Not surely the relativising of absolute standards, nor the construction of a semi-Freudian ethic to rationalise away our inhibitions. The most urgent necessity today is to start taking seriously the good news of the Holy Spirit indwelling the Church with power and glory; so that, while the Church thanks God for all the ways in which He has appeared to it and glorified His name in the past, far more it reaches out towards the future, realising that there are signs and wonders still, that still Christ is stronger than the enemy, that still where sin abounds grace much more abounds, and that still across this darkened earth there rings the music of the redeemed, the new colossal chorus of the morning stars singing together and the sons of God shouting for joy.

It is this that differentiates a dynamic infectious faith from the dull tedium of conventional religion. And it is this that differentiates a living Church from a dead ecclesiastical machine—this tension of expectancy, this urgent waiting upon God, this wondering what God will do next. 'I have both glorified My name, and will glorify it again.' And if you will receive it, this is the word of the Lord for you. Expect great things from God!

And now, coming right home to ourselves, what of this Congregation at its anniversary? God has indeed glorified His name here in years gone by. The very walls of this sanctuary are hallowed by the prayers and praises of generations. Here little children have loved to come, and youth has made its covenant with Christ; here the strong have renewed their strength and the sorrowful have received comfort; here age has found rest and light at eventide. Here has been realised the presence of a reality beyond this world, a mysterious recreating energy and refreshing grace. Across the years, there must have been thousands of people for whom this church and its services have kept the windows open towards the unseen Jerusalem, thousands who have been held to the path of rectitude and honour by memories of hours when God met them in this holy place, bringing to strengthen them for their pilgrimage the bread of life and the wine of heaven.

But surely God today is summoning you not to the past but to the future. You stand between your forefathers and your sons' sons. You know the past, you stand in the present, but God only can see the Church of the future. Not long before he died, Dr.

Alexander Whyte of St. George's declared: 'I may not live to see it—but the day will come when there will be a great revival over the whole earth.' What if that day should be now? What if, even in these days of dark and deadly menace, the dawn is breaking and we are standing again in the morning of the world? What if to you, this anniversary day, there comes from the throne of God the proclamation—'I have glorified My name in your Church's life and witness, and now I will glorify it again'? If you will receive it, this the word of the Lord for you. Expect great things from God!

One thing remains to be said. When a Congregation has existed through the generations, the greater part of its fellowship comes to be across the river on the immortal side of death. Have not the words of our text something to tell us of the life eternal? Remember that when the voice from heaven spoke to Jesus He was face to face with death. 'I have glorified My name,' said the Father: that was the Galilean ministry. 'I will glorify it again': that was Calvary with the resurrection light behind it. Surely, then, there is a message here about the journey's end and the hereafter.

This present life has brought us so much of the goodness of God that we cling to it; we are loath to contemplate parting from it. We want to turn the moving camp into a permanent abode, the desert bivouac into an abiding city. We try to fortify our brief encampment with the ramparts of material security, with the defences of health and friends and good success. We shiver when we hear the wind blowing up from the cold Jordan. Who ever, cried Gray in his *Elegy*,

> Left the warm precincts of the cheerful day,
> Nor cast one longing, ling'ring look behind?

But over against that mood I would set these words of Richard Baxter's—words which the Church has sung for three hundred years, and will still be singing long after all of us here have gone and others have taken our place:

Come, Lord, when grace hath made me meet
  Thy blessed face to see;
For, if Thy work on earth be sweet,
  What will Thy glory be?

If this life, with all its difficulties and problems, has been so wonderfully good in the lovingkindness of God, how surpassingly good it must be yonder in the sunshine of eternity! 'Eye has not seen,' declares Paul, 'nor ear heard, nor heart of man conceived what God has prepared.'

And you who may have had to say goodbye to someone you loved the best, will you listen to the trumpet-notes of your own faith? 'Christ is risen. He has abolished death. He has led captivity captive. As in Adam all die, so in Christ shall all be made alive.' This is no myth. The Greeks had a fable of a man who in old age was given back his youth. But there is nothing mythical here. For this is true. 'I have glorified My name': God did that indeed when He first brought your loved one to your side. But listen when your heart is quiet, and you will hear the voice go on, like trumpets sounding the reveille of the resurrection—'And I will glorify it again. I will give you the ecstasy of reunion, where there is no parting again for ever.'

I am persuaded you can trust a God like that. I know that you can trust Him even with the dear ones whom death has snatched away.

And when your own hour comes, that hour of which you have sometimes wondered 'How shall I do in the swellings of Jordan?' I shall tell you how you will do. When the waves are washing your soul into glory, you will hear voices shout the praises of Jesus: and then suddenly, the incredible miracle—you will be 'like Him'. Dare to imagine it—yourself, myself, like Jesus: for we shall see Him as He is.

'I have glorified My name, and will glorify it again.' Therefore —expect great things from God!

XVI

SEEING THE INVISIBLE

For the Festival of All Saints

'He endured, as seeing Him who is invisible'—Hebrews 11:27.

Today stands in the calendar of the Christian year as All Saints' Day. Who are the saints? There are three distinct meanings the word has been given.

In the first place, the Church sometimes thinks of the saints as certain outstanding men and women of God in every age—not only people who have been officially canonised but many others of holy and humble heart. Again, we often tend to think of the saints as those who have fought the good fight, and finished the course, and kept the faith, dear ones we ourselves were linked to in a lifelong union, who have gone on before us into light and joy: 'For all the saints who from their labours rest.' Once again, the New Testament normally thinks of the saints as all the people of God, the new Israel, the redeemed humanity, frail, creaturely, sinful folk who nevertheless know themselves to be committed to God in Christ—in Paul's words, 'called to be saints'.

So this is a day that does not leave out any of us. We are all in this together.

Now here is a question worth pondering. In our vocation as Christians, in our 'call to be saints' in the New Testament sense of the word, is there something we can learn from those whose lives have been an inspiration and a challenge and a rebuke, shining souls who have been joyful, courageous and triumphant where so many of us are dull and pusillanimous and defeatist?

Consider it in this way. What would you say is the essential characteristic of a saint? Certainly not any cloistered virtue. Not any remote forbidding righteousness or stereotyped piety. Probably not even what we generally think of as 'saintliness'—for in point of fact the saints have always recognised themselves as among the chief of sinners. But if there is one quality which, amid all their startling diversity, binds them together it is this. The saint is a person who has seen with piercing clarity a reality of which most of us have but a dim and blurred awareness, and who therefore believes with passion and with every atom of his being what others are content to believe vaguely and conventionally and at second hand. He knows the unseen realities which we grope after blindly. In him Christ's words are realised: 'Abide in Me, and I in you.' It is this that supernaturalises the saints beyond the levels of ordinary human nature—the fact that they are vividly alive to the existence of an unseen world all round them, and vitally aware of its supporting pressure. In the words of our text: 'They endure as seeing Him who is invisible.'

This is the great secret. And this is where All Saints' Day comes in to challenge you and me. For it means that when we are up against life's difficulties and distresses what we need most of all if we are to face these things unflinchingly is not (as the world might tell you) a tough constitution, nor a phlegmatic, imperturbable temperament, nor a psychological readjustment, nor even an approving conscience and a sense of having right on one's side. What we need most is precisely a great sense of the unseen. It is the man who is conscious of living not in one world but in two, who knows that beyond this visible environment there is an invisible realm pressing in upon him all the time, who has been granted some vision of the living Christ and entered into some experience of union with Him—this is the man who will stand fast, though the world should crash and fall. 'He endures, as seeing Him who is invisible.'

Towards the close of her brief life Emily Brontë, in a very moving little poem, made this prayer:

> Yes, as my swift days near their goal,
> 'Tis all that I implore:
> In life and death, a chainless soul,
> With courage to endure.

A chainless soul, unfettered by time and chance and circumstance, with courage to endure and to stand unflinching in the face of life's sharp, testing hours—is not this a cry which, even if inarticulately, comes sooner or later to the lips of all? And the Word of God is here today to tell us of an answer. To see the King in His beauty—this is the real secret of possessing a chainless soul. 'He endured'—he stood unflinching—'as seeing Him who is invisible.'

Let us, on this All Saints' Day, try to apprehend this truth, not abstractly, but in action. It would no doubt be possible to prove by abstract reasoning that the unseen things of life are every whit as real as, indeed far more so than, the things we see; that it is only an interpretation of life in terms of the unseen that makes sense of the universe; and that the difficulties in the way of consistent scepticism and unbelief about the unseen are far more serious and insurmountable than the difficulties in the way of consistent faith. But today let us follow a different line. I propose to take four concrete experiences in the lives of all of us, four familiar difficult experiences we encounter on our journey through the world; and I am going to ask you to observe how four great men of God, facing these crucial experiences, conquered and overcame—because they saw something, or rather Someone, the world could not see, precisely by their hold upon the unseen. 'They endured, as seeing Him who is invisible.' May God make this come true of us!

The first test of endurance is all that hurting side of life which might be summed up under the word *Discipline*: what the Bible calls chastisement. 'Whom the Lord loves He chastens'—He disciplines—'and scourges every son whom He receives'. We all get our share of this: the cutting edge of sorrow; the wear and tear of tasks beyond our strength; the discipline of adversity, of frustration, of hopes indefinitely deferred; the discipline of fierce temptation. Many a time, under such experience, faith flinches and endurance breaks.

Let us find our picture for this. We do not need to search far for it. We shall take the man about whom the words in our text were originally spoken. Take Moses in Egypt.

Here was this Hebrew Greatheart on fire to save his nation. Here was this impetuous spirit who had been known on one occasion to turn upon a ruthless Egyptian slave-driver and strike him dead. Such was the hot, vehement stuff of which this man was made. And for years his one thought was—'I must get my people out of here! I must free them from this vast concentration camp of Egypt. It is intolerable that this totalitarian tyranny should triumph, and freedom perish from the earth!' And God came to him, saying in effect—'Moses, wait! You must bide My appointed time. The hour is not yet!'

How did the man take this discipline of waiting and unfulfilment? Did he retort—'Wait? When I am sick and tired of waiting? When Egypt's bondage is slowly strangling our national existence, and every day is driving the iron deeper into my people's soul?' Many a man would have railed at providence. But not this man. For beyond the harsh, daunting incubus of Egypt he had seen something alive, a sentinel Figure in the background, God moving behind the shadows keeping watch above His own. 'He endured, as seeing Him who is invisible.'

But of course that was not all. It was not only the discipline of passive waiting that Moses endured. There was the fiercer discipline of active temptation. Did you notice the words? 'Choosing rather to suffer affliction with the people of God, than to enjoy the pleasures of sin for a season; esteeming the reproach of Christ greater riches than the treasures in Egypt.' The Egyptian government proposed collaboration. They held out glittering prizes, if only he would consent to drop his moral intransigence. They said in effect—'Man, don't be a fool! Tone down your standards. Be broadminded! Be realistic, and face the facts. You are in Egypt now; do as the Egyptians do! Pharaoh offers you a pact, an honourable pact. Come now, what do you say?' And I can see Moses rising up like a man in wrath. 'What do I say? I say, Go back to your master, and fling that word honour in his teeth! Where is the honour of going with the crowd and abjuring the discipline of God? Tell Pharaoh my word for him is this: Get behind me, Satan! I have seen a greater King than Pharaoh on the throne, the Lord God omnipotent reigning!'

So this man endured his discipline—of waiting and of temptation—as seeing Him who is invisible. And when we have to endure this double discipline—when we have to wait for our dreams to be fulfilled, and there is no sign of the things we have set our heart on coming true, and the triumph of truth seems to tarry till we are sick with hope deferred; and when we meet the fiercer discipline of temptation, when some minor manipulation of conscience will ease and facilitate the road, or when you have the apostles of a new secular culture dinning it into a generation's ears that the reproach of Christ is a poor kind of exchange for the treasures of Egypt—at such a time there is only one sure safeguard and defence, and that is to see past the immediate show of things, past the materialist philosophy which blindly thinks this world is all, to see past that to the unseen environment, throbbing and beating all around us, in which we live and move and have our being, and of which, with Francis Thompson, we can say

> O world invisible, we view thee,
> O world intangible, we touch thee,
> O world unknowable, we know thee,
> Inapprehensible, we clutch thee—

and to see as the very heart and centre of that world the living God, revealed to us in Jesus Christ. God give us that vision of the saints for the day of discipline, that like them we too may endure as seeing Him who is invisible.

A second test of endurance is *Danger*. There is a formidable element of danger, of sheer physical risk, in life today. Our tenure of health, of happiness, of life itself—who can be sure of it? The doctor says one day, 'This is going to be a dangerous operation.' The politician says, 'We have to learn to live dangerously in this atomic age.' The economist says, 'There is always the danger of an economic blizzard and bankruptcy.' So many of our old securities have gone with the wind of world wars and economic revolutions; and no one knows what may be coming on the earth. Is there any spiritual panoply for the day of danger?

Let us take a second Scripture scene. Take Elisha and his young servant at Dothan. It was early one morning. The night before, there had been rumours of invasion, tales of enemy troops seen closing in from all directions. In the grey light of dawn, the younger man had climbed the hill to scan the countryside. He came running back with his tidings. He burst in breathless on Elisha. 'Master, what shall we do? The worst has happened! They are all round us—the Syrians. I saw the dawn light flashing on a thousand chariots and ten thousand spears. They have us in a trap. We are done for. We shall never get out of here alive!'

What has Elisha to say to that? He has this to say: 'Fear not'—and the words come out with the ring of trumpets in them—'fear not; they that be with us are more than they that be with them.'

Whereupon, I suppose, the younger man looked at him in angry astonishment. 'But Elisha, master, you do not know what you are saying! You have not seen them. I have. They have whole battalions—and we have no one. This place is quite defenceless. Why mock me by telling me that they who are with us are more than those who are with them? Surely it is no time for jesting!'

But Elisha did not argue with him. He bowed his head and prayed. 'Lord, I pray Thee, open his eyes, that he may see.' As much as to say, 'O God, here is a man who cannot endure this hour of danger—unless he sees the invisible. Lord, help him!'

And the prayer was answered. For from the servant's lips came a cry—'I see it! I see it! The mountain is full of horses and chariots of fire round about us!'

Do not dare to call that sham or sophistry. We become so obsessed with things seen and temporal, so dominated in our thinking by the grim, immediate problems that stand menacingly athwart our path. Earth may be crammed with heaven, and every common bush afire with God: but so often we can see nothing but the hills round Dothan and the Syrians camping in the valley, nothing but the vast dangers with which our civilisation is encompassed and the dire threat to everything we cherish and hold dear. And the great work of faith is just to stab dull spirits broad awake to the unseen environment: for there Christ sits enthroned, Kings of kings and Lord of lords for ever.

The Bible does not say, mark you, that God will eliminate the danger. It does not necessarily promise that kind of safety. The Syrians may still be mustering their fierce array at Dothan's gates. The doctor may still say that it is going to be a dangerous operation. The politician may still talk of the danger of an economic blizzard. The principalities and powers may still be plotting another devastating assault on the basic freedoms of the world. Even the Church may be driven underground, as in the days of the catacombs. God does not necessarily remove the peril. He does something infinitely better. He opens our eyes to let us see the total reality of things: and the reality of things is God's ring of fire all round the mountain; and round our mortal weakness, rank upon serried rank of the shining hosts of heaven.

> Let troubles rise, and terrors frown,
> And days of darkness fall;
> Through Him all dangers we'll defy,
> And more than conquer all.

'Through Him'—the dear Saviour of us all. May God give us this vision of the saints for the day of danger, that we like them may endure as seeing Him who is invisible.

The third test of endurance is *Disillusionment*. Multitudes of people at this hour are feeling desperately disillusioned. Disillusioned about the international situation. Disillusioned about the brave new world for which men fought and died. Disillusioned about the Church and the prospects of the Kingdom of God. Disillusioned about themselves, and about the early ideals which the corroding years have blighted and destroyed. Who does not know something of the dark menace of this experience? It can make the heart flinch and endurance break.

So now I give you a third picture. Take Isaiah. Take the experience which turned Isaiah into a prophet. He began as a young courtier at the royal court, complacent and content. On the throne of Judah sat Uzziah, the greatest monarch the land had seen since Solomon. And the young courtier was carefree and secure, absorbed in the duties of his immediate environment, fascinated by the material splendours all around him, quite sure that this wealth and glory and stability were bound to last for ever.

But there came a day when the sunshine of that splendour was suddenly veiled and shrouded. A strange rumour went throughout the land. Men stopped one another in the streets and spoke of it in whispers. 'Have you heard? Our great Uzziah! He is struck down with leprosy. How are the mighty fallen! The king —a leper!' And then, as though that shadow across the nation's sky were not darkness enough, out of the east came looming like a gigantic thundercloud the baleful spectre of Assyria. Then, suddenly, the deepening of the crisis, the news flying round the capital—'The king is dead! The Assyrian is at the gates!'

Isaiah, the young courtier, hearing that, felt as though his life were being torn from its moorings. Everything he had trusted in, everything that had been his world so solid and substantial and indispensable, all the philosophy of life he had built upon— just crashed into chaos round him. It was disillusionment, catastrophic and complete.

In that bitter hour, his steps led him—he hardly knew why— to the precincts of the temple. It is a good place for any dis- illusioned heart. And there it was that destiny, vivid and dramatic, burst upon him. For there, on that day when all the visible pomp and circumstance of earth had failed him, and all the marvellous good times had vanished into dust, his eyes beheld the glory of the coming of the Lord. 'In the year that king Uzziah died,' he wrote, describing it afterwards, 'I saw'—hark how that note comes again, beating through the narrative, that same tremendous note of vision—'I saw the Lord, high and lifted up! I found there was a whole world I had been ignoring. My blindness was pierced, my darkness scattered. I saw the Lord!' And from that moment the badly shattered, disillusioned young courtier was a man inspired, reaching out eager arms of dedication towards that world unseen: 'Here am I, Lord. Here am I—send me!'

Disillusioned, are we, about the world? Disillusioned about humanity? Disillusioned about our own poor worthless lives? Indeed, God knows we have reason for it. We have seen so many Utopian dreams scattered and shattered and in ruin. But it is precisely here that faith can go into action redeemingly. Faith is the higher realism which adds on a new dimension, a sixth sense, the faculty of spiritual vision. 'In the year when king Uzziah died'—in the day when all I had ever trusted in went bankrupt and the dream faded into disenchantment and I knew

the colossal helplessness of man, in that day I saw the Lord: I
had my narrow horizons stretched to include the unseen and
eternal. What right have I to be so disenchanted about the world
that I forget the sovereignty of my Saviour? There is always far
more in Christ to make me hopeful and rejoicing than there can
be anywhere else in the world to make me disillusioned and
defeated. May God give us this vision of the saints for the day
of disillusionment, that we too may endure as seeing Him who is
invisible.

We have looked, then, at these three critical days in life—
the day of discipline, the day of danger, the day of disillusionment—and have observed how in every case the vision of the
unseen is the secret of endurance. One final day awaits us all:
the day of *Death*. How shall we do in the swellings of Jordan?

I must leave you to fill in the details of this last picture for
yourselves: but here it is, in a couple of strokes. The streets of
Jerusalem. A mad mob shouting. A brave young martyr dying.
His name is Stephen, his crime the preaching of the gospel, his
punishment a hail of flying stones. 'Death to the heretic!' they
are shouting. 'Beat the life out of him. Silence him for ever!'
And now beneath that whirling torrent the man has fallen on
his knees, and his head is bowed, and the blood is streaming into
his eyes, and the end is very near: when suddenly, startling
them all, so that the stones fall from their hands, he gazes up,
and for a moment the poor bruised, disfigured face is like the face
of an angel; and then, a great cry that echoes and re-echoes—
'I see heaven opened'—always that note of seeing the unseen—
'I see heaven opened, and the Son of Man standing at the right
hand of God. Jesus, Jesus, Jesus, I come to Thee!'

Fear death, when death comes one day for you? You need
have no fear of it, any more than your own dear ones feared it
when it came. It will be no dark ominous spectre you see coming then to meet you. It will be the King in His beauty.

> Jesus, Lover of my soul,
> Let me to Thy bosom fly.

Do you remember John Bunyan's marvellous description in the

Pilgrim's Progress of the summons to Mr. Valiant-for-truth to cross the river? 'When the day that he must go hence was come, many accompanied him to the river side, into which as he went he said, "Death, where is thy sting?" And as he went down deeper, he said, "Grave, where is thy victory?" So he passed over, and all the trumpets sounded for him on the other side.' May God give us that vision of the saints for the day of death, that like them we too, in that final hour—in that hour supremely —may endure as seeing Him who is invisible. And then, that day over and that river crossed, we shall indeed see Him face to face, and rejoice in His presence for ever.

XVII

THE DESIRE OF ALL NATIONS

An Advent Sermon

'All the ends of the earth shall see the salvation of our God'—Isaiah 52:10.

I am going to ask you to co-operate with me in this sermon today in one particular way. I want you to make a special act of imagination. But first, let us start by getting the main thesis clear. Quite briefly, it is this.

The one hope of the world today lies in the Advent message: Immanuel, God with us, God in Christ reconciling the world. But the world keeps looking in other directions. Some are looking to political institutions and developments to fashion a new earth; some to culture and technology; some to humanitarian enterprise and ethical endeavour. We need all that indeed: of course we need it. But unless there is a surer foundation, we are heading ultimately for disillusionment. The basic need is not man's confident self-sufficiency, but God's redemptive action; not just more human planning on the horizontal level, but the inrush of a divine creative power from the beyond. Whether the world knows it or not, Christ is still today as ever the Desire of all nations, the one Hope of the ends of the earth.

Now this is what I propose to do, and it is here I ask for your imaginative co-operation. I want you to imagine yourselves back into the very end of the pre-Christian era, the time we designate B.C. In fact, I want you to imagine that it is precisely one year before the birth of Christ. And you and I are going on a journey. We are going to visit in turn three great cities—Rome, Athens, Jerusalem. And in these cities we are going to overhear three conversations, three groups of typical men discussing their hopes and fears for the world in that particular year—just one year before the birth of Christ. Perhaps we shall find that our own hopes and fears are strangely mirrored there.

First, then, come with me to the city of Rome, the capital of the world. I want you to imagine a room in an officers' club in Rome. Three junior officers of Caesar's army—we shall call them Gaius, Cassius, Octavius—have met there and are talking together. They are discussing new postings for overseas military service which have just been announced that day. Gaius is speaking.

GAIUS: So you are going off, Cassius, with the next draft to Asia; and you, Octavius, to the forgotten legion among the wild Germanic tribes of the far north. I am luckier then either of you. I am for Carthage and North Africa. The gods only know when we shall meet again. Tell me, Cassius, do you like this overseas service?

CASSIUS: Like it, Gaius? I hate it! But what can you do? It is the penalty of belonging to so great an Empire. It is the price of being a citizen of the master-race. That is what we owe to Caesar. Did you hear, Gaius, the terms of Caesar's latest edict? Listen to this: 'There has gone forth a decree from Caesar Augustus that all the world should be taxed.' These were the very words. 'All the world'! That is our Empire. That is why you have to go to Africa, Gaius, and you, Octavius, to the tribes beyond the Rhine, and myself to Asia. All the ends of the earth have seen the might of Caesar. Do you know what they are calling Caesar now? I heard them shouting it as he drove down to the Colosseum yesterday. The air was ringing with it. It was not only 'Augustus' now. They were shouting—'Caesar! Hail to the divine Caesar! Hail, Son of God, Saviour of the world!' Was that not fine, Octavius?

OCTAVIUS: Fine? I wonder. Saviour of the world! Caesar? No doubt he has given us the *pax Romana*: but what is that, when all is said and done? A subtle manipulation of the balance of power, with the legions massed on the frontiers. The thing looks secure, built to last a thousand years—but don't you trust it. The foundations are creaking. I tell you, the glittering civilisation we are so proud of is disintegrating, and it will take more than Caesar to stop the rot. That revolt of the slaves a few years back, for instance—that was symptomatic. Oh, I know they crucified the lot, and silenced them: but it showed what is coming. And I ask you, Cassius and Gaius, is it right that there should be a million slaves? Is it right that with all the resources of civilisation at our disposal there should still be these sub-human conditions? Is it right that life should be so horribly cheap? There was Quirinus the other day. They wanted a son in that family, and when the baby was born it was a girl; and they threw the child out to die. Is that right? This shining civilisation of ours—are there not in it the seeds of its own corruption and decay and death? What do you say, Gaius?

GAIUS: I say, Octavius, you are mad to talk like that. Do you not know that if Rome relaxed its hold the world would fall to pieces? Do you not see that if you liberate the slaves you wreck the State? Am I not right, Cassius?

CASSIUS: Of course you are, Gaius. Don't you get playing with these revolutionary ideas, Octavius! In any case, you will not find any support—unless it be from some of those meddling Jews: Pompey was a fool ever to bring them here to Rome, but Caesar will see to that. Augustus knows what he is about. He has this cosmopolitan crowd under his thumb. 'Bread and circuses'—that is all they want; as long as they have bread to eat, and circuses to amuse them, they ask no more. Can't you see that, Octavius?

OCTAVIUS: No, Cassius, I can't. Bread and circuses—do you think man can really live on that? He wants more. He wants life. He wants freedom. He wants spiritual fulfilment. I tell you, Cassius, he wants God!

CASSIUS: Just Listen, Gaius, to our very religious captain! He tells us we need God. Well, even that Caesar has given us. Has Caesar himself not been raised to the rank of divinity? You and I, of course, do not believe it: we know it is just political expediency. Caesar himself does not believe it. But the man in the street does believe it, and it hoaxes him all right. This emperor-worship keeps men quiet—and what else is religion for? Do you agree, Gaius?

GAIUS: Yes, heartily. I tell you, Octavius, that crowd at the Colosseum was right. Caesar is indeed the saviour of the world: and if you want peace on earth, goodwill among men, power-politics are the way to achieve it. Nothing else can do it.

OCTAVIUS: You are wrong, Gaius! I know you are wrong. I had a dream one night. It was when I was away last year with the Fifteenth Legion building the great new military road across Macedonia to the east. One night I had this dream. I dreamt another army was using the road we had made: an army coming out of the east to match its power with Caesar. A strange army it was—peasants, artisans, fisherfolk, slaves. And on their banners they had, what do you think? A gallows-tree! A cross! And they spoke of another Emperor, both God and man in one, the Desire of all nations, dead, resurrected, alive for ever. And nothing could stop them. I saw them reaching Rome. I saw them casting down the throne of Caesar. I saw their all-conquering Commander taking his place. Then I awoke, and it was a dream. But—Gaius, Cassius—I believe God sent it. I think it meant that power-politics have had their day. I am sure this strange new Emperor will be the Saviour of the world.

Now we leave Rome. We pass on to Athens. I want you to imagine three dons of the university of Athens, members of the Hellenic Academy of philosophy and the sciences, having a walk together on the Areopagus and conversing as they go. We shall call them Ariston, Leonidas and Dionysius. Remember it is still precisely one year before the birth of Christ. Ariston is the speaker.

ARISTON: I hear you had a famous triumph in the debate last night, Leonidas. What was it all about?

LEONIDAS: Well, Ariston, it was about the ideal society, the new order we have all been talking about for the last four hundred years, ever since Plato wrote his *Republic*. The actual title of the debate was 'Can Culture Save the World?'

ARISTON: And you led for the affirmative, Leonidas? Who took the negative?

LEONIDAS: It was Thrasymachus. You know him? He is a melancholy dog. His argument amounted to this, that if culture could have saved the world, then why did Plato and Pericles not save it centuries ago? A fallacy, of course!

ARISTON: Indeed, Leonidas, a glaring fallacy. And what did you say?

LEONIDAS : Oh, I took the line that Plato and Aristotle laid the foundation, but that the new knowledge has to permeate the general mind—which means universal education. I pointed out that we are moving in that direction: witness the fact that we have a universal language now. The Greek tongue will carry you anywhere in the world today. What a chance, by the way, for the missionaries of any new world religion, if one should ever appear! I pointed out that little by little we are banishing ignorance, that we are translating knowledge into practical resources for living, that indeed there is no limit to what scientific enlightenment and intellectual energy may achieve. And, Ariston, with the last words of my peroration, I quite brought down the house!

ARISTON : I am sure you did, Leonidas. What were your last words?

LEONIDAS : They were these: 'The mind of man the only Saviour of the world!' Oh yes, it was a good debate; and when they took the vote, a splendid triumph—one hundred and seventy votes to forty-five, no doubt about it! You should have been there, Ariston; and you, too, Dionysius. You seem very quiet today, Dionysius. You don't challenge my argument, do you?

DIONYSIUS : Yes, Leonidas, I do. You say knowledge, culture, can save the world. I say it can't, not ever! You say knowledge is power. Yes, but power for what? Suppose a man dominated by self-interest, what is to prevent him using his power for selfish instead of benevolent ends? Nothing. What is to prevent him making intelligence, culture, truth itself the accomplice of evil? Nothing. So that all your argument in the debate last night, Leonidas, goes to pieces on one rock—the fact of evil: and that is a fact which not all your logic can rationalise away. You are a philosopher, Leonidas. You must see the truth of what I am saying.

LEONIDAS : Yes, Dionysius, I think I do. But what is the alternative? If you rule out culture and enlightenment as the saviour of the world, what are you to put in its place? Force— like those imperial masters of ours in Rome?

DIONYSIUS : No, Leonidas, certainly not force!

LEONIDAS : Well then, Dionysius, if salvation can come neither from the war-lords at Rome nor from the Academy at Athens, where is it to come from? You are not suggesting we should look to Olympus, are you? We have a whole pantheon of gods there to choose from—Zeus, Athene, Artemis, Apollo, all the bickering hierarchy of heaven. Why, our very Acropolis is stuffed full of their statues: and I reckon that one day sooner or later we shall be erecting—just in case any deity should have been inadvertently overlooked—an altar inscribed 'To the Unknown God'! This multiplicity of gods is the satire of every cheap comedian. You are not suggesting surely that we should be credulous enough to make our prayer to them? Are you, Dionysius?

DIONYSIUS: No, Leonidas, I do not mean that. But listen! You have read your Homer. You have heard Homer tell of gods like Apollo coming down to earth in human form. That is myth, of course. There is no salvation there. But just think, Leonidas, think, Ariston, what if the great Spirit Himself, the First Cause and Creator of the universe, what if He took flesh and came amongst us, and shared with us His Spirit, His infinite power, His eternal life? Would there not be salvation in that? What do you think, Leonidas?

LEONIDAS: Oh, Dionysius, if it could only be! How wonderful! The great God Himself, walking this very earth, strengthening our weakness, guiding and supporting our pilgrim way—the Healer and the Saviour of the world!

Now just once more we are moving on. From Rome and Athens we pass on to Jerusalem. We enter one of the porches of the temple. We are to imagine three men talking there, in that same first year before the birth of Christ—at the very time when Gaius, Cassius and Octavius were discoursing in their officers' club in Rome, and Ariston, Leonidas and Dionysius on the slopes of Areopagus at Athens—three Jews conversing in the temple at Jerusalem, a priest, a scribe, and a Rabbi. We shall call them Abner the priest, Baruch the scribe, and Joseph the Rabbi. Baruch the scribe is speaking.

BARUCH: I love that psalm we had at morning prayers today, the longest and greatest of them all. Its words keep ringing in my ears. Do you remember? 'Oh how I love Thy law! It is my meditation all the day.' If men would only love God's law, and practise its precepts of brotherhood and goodwill and mutual kindness, all our troubles would be solved. Salvation is such a simple thing: keep the law, and earn God's favour; do good works, and merit heaven. And if you fall, there is always the ritual of the sacrifices to put you right again. That is your part, Abner. You are a priest.

ABNER: Yes, Baruch, if your lifework is the law, mine is the sacrificial system. Our fathers gave us everything when they gave us these: the law and the sacrifices—the salvation of the world. But Rabbi Joseph, why are you frowning? Do you not agree?

JOSEPH: Listen, Abner! Listen, Baruch! You have the law and the sacrifices: are you content with the result? I am not. Here am I, a Rabbi, a religious man: but I know that my life, my character, are far, far short of what they ought to be. And you— are you never disappointed? Never frustrated? Is the good always victorious—in you? Can you say that, honestly? Oh, why are we all so impotent? Can you tell me that, Abner, priest of God?

ABNER: Speak for yourself, Rabbi Joseph! I do not admit the impeachment. I am a righteous man. I thank God I am. I fast twice in the week. I give tithes of all I possess. I am quite satisfied with my record.

JOSEPH: Are you really, Abner? Are you sure you are not running away from the truth about yourself? Have you ever faced yourself with all pretences down? You are so proud of your good works. That is precisely the trouble: good works and pride, always hand in hand. And pride is the cardinal sin. So that our very good works, our very obediences to the law, are our undoing. This is the vicious circle, Abner; and neither your sacrifices nor Baruch's law can break it. Baruch, do you not see that this is true?

BARUCH: I see, Joseph, that you are becoming much too subtle. Besides, you are forgetting something. What about the Messiah? You don't imagine that Messiah, when He comes, is going to trouble about your bits of sins, and mine, and Abner's? He will have more to do than that! He is coming to deal with those Roman usurpers of our liberties, coming to consign the whole hateful crew to Gehenna. Down with Rome and up with Jewry —that is what I say! That is the kind of Saviour Israel needs. Rabbi Joseph, face the facts!

JOSEPH: Yes, Baruch, and the more I face them the more

I see that your saviour will never save the world. Not through that kind of Messiah will man's inward spiritual nature find renewal. Above everything else we need forgiveness. We need cleansing. We need the power of a new nature. And Abner, all your religious observances cannot do it. Baruch, all your moral effort is hopeless. If the human predicament is ever to be resolved, God alone must do it. But think, Abner, when you talk about sacrifice, just think—what if God Himself should make the sacrifice? Think, Baruch, when you quote your psalms about the law, think what another psalmist says: 'If I make my bed in hell, behold Thou art there!' Surely if God in very truth were to come and meet us there, the great God humbling Himself for our sakes to the lowest depths, nothing could stand against that! It would be the routing of every darkness and the ending of every night. All things would be made new. O come, Redeemer of the race! Come now, O Saviour of the world!

Our journey is over. We have been to Rome, Athens, Jerusalem, one year before the birth of Christ. But you know that what we have encountered there is just ourselves today. Their hopes and fears are ours here and now. For still some look to power and government for the saving of the world; and some to knowledge and enlightenment; and some to the self-sufficiency of the morally religious man. But through it all, the human heart, unhealed, stands crying for a better deliverance.

What then? Why should we Christians so often seem to be on the wrong side of the Advent still? We are not living B.C. now. We are living A.D. This is the year of the Lord. This is the Day of the Lord. This is the House of the Lord. And God is most certainly here. We are most blessed. He is here in Christ. In Christ, He has reconciled us to Himself. In Christ, He is reconciling the world. Even where He is quite unknown, in Christ He is working out the purposes of His Kingdom: and 'all the ends of the earth shall see the salvation of our God'. We see not yet the ending of the problems and perplexities—individual, social, international—that keep crowding in upon us. But we see Jesus, the Desire of all nations, the Hope of the ends of the earth, the one dear Saviour of us all. In the faith of Christ, let us go out now and through all the tomorrows that yet will be, to live for Him and to share His gospel with the world—until the day break, and the shadows flee away.

Our glad hosannas, Prince of Peace,
Thy welcome shall proclaim;
And heaven's eternal arches ring
With Thy belovèd name.